The Dark Side of
East London

This book is dedicated to the members of the Tower Hamlets Walkshop, a group which is working to develop a structured guiding culture in the London Borough of Tower Hamlets.

The group is creating guided tours in the less obvious parts of the borough in order to explore and share the rich heritage of the Tower Hamlets, an area with a long and complex story.

One of the members is Alan Tucker whose photographs, taken especially to illustrate this book, locate the following stories in today's East End.

The Dark Side of East London

David Charnick

PEN & SWORD HISTORY

First published in Great Britain in 2016 by
PEN AND SWORD HISTORY
an imprint of
Pen and Sword Books Ltd
47 Church Street
Barnsley
South Yorkshire S70 2AS

ISBN 978 1 47385 644 8

Printed and bound in England
by CPI Group (UK) Ltd, Croydon, CR0 4YY

Typeset in Times New Roman by
CHIC GRAPHICS

Pen & Sword Books Ltd incorporates the imprints of Pen & Sword
Archaeology, Atlas, Aviation, Battleground, Discovery,
Family History, History, Maritime, Military, Naval, Politics, Railways,
Select, Social History, Transport, True Crime, Claymore Press,
Frontline Books, Leo Cooper, Praetorian Press, Remember When,
Seaforth Publishing and Wharncliffe.

For a complete list of Pen and Sword titles please contact
Pen and Sword Books Limited
47 Church Street, Barnsley, South Yorkshire, S70 2AS, England
E-mail: enquiries@pen-and-sword.co.uk
Website: www.pen-and-sword.co.uk

Contents

Illustrations

Introduction

Old Sins Cast Long Shadows

On the south-western corner of the churchyard of St Matthew, Bethnal Green, there is a small building. Constructed in 1754 and extended in 1826 to accommodate a fire-engine, it is the only one of Bethnal Green's two watch houses to survive. The other, on the east side of the parish near the Green itself, has long since disappeared. The watch house was relocated here from the junction of what are now Bethnal Green Road and Brick Lane so that the watch could keep an eye on the graves to prevent body snatching. It was on the pavement outside this watch house that a woman was left by the watch to die of exposure, one of their many misuses of power which helped pave the way in the 1820s for Robert Peel's Metropolitan Police Act.[1]

Ann Ashley
At about two o'clock on a cold, rainy Wednesday morning in November 1825, a woman called Ann Ashley was found in the gutter by a watchman. Much the worse for drink, she was also soaking wet from the rain. The watchman hauled her to the watch house where Constable Simkins took over. Though he didn't charge her he did put her in the cell, which from descriptions of it as a 'hole' and a 'dungeon' was presumably below ground level. It should be remembered that as well as being wet and cold, she had been drinking; alcohol increases the susceptibility to cold.

Ann was left in the cell to shiver while Simkins and his men were nice and warm before the fire. At five o'clock, when the watch house keeper came off duty, she was taken out and dumped on the pavement outside. By this time she was far too ill to stand, so she was left to sit on the cold ground until about nine o'clock when she was taken to the workhouse, the only place in Bethnal Green where an infirmary could be found. She was dead on arrival.

The inquest into her death was heard the following Saturday before coroner John Wright Unwin at the *King and Queen* pub on the corner of Hare (now Cheshire) Street and Wood Close. Unwin himself died just five years later, at the age of 58. During the hearing one of the jury suggested a visit to see the cell where Ann was confined. Accordingly, the jury went to the nearby watch house to investigate. They found what *The Examiner* later called a 'horrible hole' and a 'diabolical purgatory', describing the cell as:

> *about six feet square, with a damp gravelly floor, and reeking with the smell of human excrement to such a degree that it is really astonishing that any person who had been confined there, even but for an hour, could escape contagion.*

Another contemporary source announced that Ann was thrown into a 'sink of pestilence' which was 'streaming with damp, and reeking with human ordure'.

At the inquest the surgeon confirmed that Ann Ashley's death had been caused by 'wet and cold, combined with intoxication'. The jury concluded that the constable and the watch should be brought to account for their neglect which, the coroner admitted, had accelerated Ann's death. However, there was a limit to what the jury could do. Though the coroner admitted that Ann Ashley's death might have been prevented by proper care on the parts of the night constable and watchmen, and that it was accelerated by the treatment she received, he had ruled at the commencement of the hearing that the evidence did not warrant a charge of manslaughter. Instead, this was to be an inquest into a misdemeanour, and no other verdict could be brought in.

The Coroner

This ruling was completely unacceptable to one journalist, who called for a proper trial for the 'brute' Simkins and his 'myrmidons', designating them 'her murderers' and 'homicides in law'. If this is not manslaughter, the article says, a judge and jury should say so. To rule that this death was the result of a misdemeanour is 'one of the grossest jests on justice we have ever heard'.

Such interference by a coroner was not without precedent. Sandra Hempel cites an inquest held in 1829 before West Middlesex coroner Joseph Carttar into the death of William Adams, aged 3 years. William died because an apothecary at the charitable Kent Dispensary had prescribed him a toxic regimen of calomel and antimony. The jury's verdict was 'death by the visitation of God', but they added that there had been culpable neglect on the part of both the apothecary and William's mother (who had left him sometimes in the care of neighbours, and sometimes alone, because she had to scrape a living by labouring). Coroner Carttar however overrode their comments: 'the apothecary's actions were no concern of theirs' because no-one could expect medical men acting for free to give much attention to non-paying patients.[2]

Carttar's ruling that William had died 'not in consequence of the neglect of any person or persons' may have something to do with his being the salaried secretary to the dispensary in question. There is no evidence to imply any such conflict of interest in Unwin's decision on the death of Ann Ashley, but the example shows that at the time coroners felt free to exert their authority. Indeed Hempel quotes the reflection of John Gordon Smith, the University of London's first Professor of Medical Jurisprudence, that 'the coroner tells the jury what to do, the jury do as they are bid, and everybody gets away in good time for dinner or supper'.[3]

Shadowy Heritage

Most people with an interest in the darker side of London life know that the William Davis Primary School, across Wood Close from the watch house, was attended by the infant Kray Twins. It is also quite well-known that the Twins were to acquire the *Carpenters' Arms* pub at the end of St Matthews Row, and that Tommy 'Ginger' Marks was shot dead outside the pub in 1965, having been set up by Freddie Foreman. But the injustice committed at the watch house and compounded in a nearby pub is relatively unknown. The *King and Queen* closed in 1996. Though converted for residential use, the building is recognisably a former pub.[4]

The saying is that old sins cast long shadows. The story of Ann Ashley is one of many stories that lurk behind the frontages of several East End buildings, or haunt many sites that have since been built over but often retain some intimation of what was there before. However, those stories are largely unheard. When asked to name shadier characters from the East End, most people come to a halt after the Kray Twins and that amorphous character Jack the Ripper. Some may have heard of Arthur Harding. But how many have heard of Benjamin Russen, serial child rapist, or Joseph Merceron, local property magnate and villain? Yet both are linked inextricably with the parish church of St Matthew, whose churchyard the watch house has guarded for over 250 years – indeed, Merceron's grave survives on the south side of the church.

This study reconstructs some of these stories: most of them are criminal; all concern the darker side of the East End. But this is not a salacious trawl through the area's seamy past. Rather, it has two principal objectives: to shed light on the development of the East End, and to show how the past is still very much present in the visible, tangible heritage which the area possesses but which tends to be neglected in favour of other parts of London.

Why Crime?
There are no doubt more 'legitimate' ways to explore local history. However, while stories of crime and the darker side of life have their attractions for a specific readership, they are also good gauges of the times in which they are set because they are anecdotal. Like ghost stories, which are themselves often the adjuncts to crime stories, they reveal aspects of human experience in situations which lead often to crisis, and shed light on the minutiae of daily life.

The usual image evoked by considering the past of the 'East End', a term current only from the 1880s, is an indistinct vision of fog-laden Victorian alleyways and slums, of dockers and costermongers, of jellied eels and shellfish stalls. But how representative of the areas east of the City is this vision? This is the question addressed by Jane Cox in her recent study *Old East Enders* which explores the story of the Tower Hamlets from prehistoric times through to the creation of the docks which transformed the area in the early nineteenth century. As she says in her introduction, public perception seems to be that 'there was no life in the East End before that era of modern folklore'. To counter this Cox explores in evocative detail the times 'when the suburbs, villages and hamlets east of the Tower were independent places, with their own identities'.[5]

This study is not the comprehensive evocation of life in the Tower Hamlets before the 'East End' which Cox presents. Instead there is a focus on the eighteenth and nineteenth centuries in order to give a flavour of the area as it was before and after it was absorbed into the new metropolis. Reconstructions of significant moments in the darker story of the areas which make up the Tower Hamlets evoke often overlooked aspects of life on what might be termed the 'other side' of the City.

Past and Present

However, these are not just moments in the past, separate from the present. London is an old city, yet also a city of the future; one of death and of life. In many ways it can be said that in London, the past and the future join hands in the present. All around London can be found in its heritage evidence of how it came to be the place it is. This does not of course mean that such heritage is understood, let alone appreciated. The present study seeks then not only to evoke the past, but also to show how close it is to the unheeding passer-by on the streets of the London Borough of Tower Hamlets.

To this end, the photographs which illustrate this book have been commissioned especially to locate the stories in the present-day East End. They show what remains on the streets to give the past a tangible link to the present. Some of the pictures, however, bear witness to how much heritage has been lost to development over time. London is a forward-looking city, which means that development is inevitable, as is the loss of some local heritage. It is, therefore, all the more important to appreciate what has survived while it is still here to be appreciated.

Chapter 1

The Cutters' Riots

It is early one December morning in 1769, and the sun will scarcely have risen when the smacking of mallets against wood begins to ring out in the cold, clean winter air, echoing across the Bethnal Green. Perhaps it intrudes into the disturbed dreamtime state of the sad, suffering inmates of Matthew Wright's madhouse on the other side of the Green. A scaffold is going up outside the *Salmon and Ball* tavern, on the Bethnal Green at the top of Dog Row; a double scaffold, raised for two men who are due to swing at eleven o'clock. One is of Irish extraction, John Doyle; the other is John Valline, a Huguenot. Both are journeyman weavers, convicted of cutting: destroying the silk on the looms of master weavers who are deemed not to pay their journeymen fairly. Both were to have been turned off at Tyburn in October, but Sir James Eyre, the Recorder of London, intervened. Being the principal judge of the City of London, he decreed that they should be hanged near the heart of the weaving trade, that their deaths might prove a grim warning.[1]

It is not surprising that a crowd is beginning to gather after the arrival of the two carts from Newgate, one containing two prisoners, one the scaffold. After all, the hangings are great entertainment for the Londoner, and a trip to Tyburn or Tower Hill is a day out in itself. But this time the crowd has not come for fun, and all too quickly it becomes clear that the crowd's mood is dangerous. This is weaving territory after all, and most of the locals are journeymen. Some of them are cutters themselves, and all of them will have been suffering from the pressures being brought to bear on the trade. As the workmen build the scaffold, their thumps are interrupted by objects hurled from within the mob, sometimes striking the wood, sometimes the workmen. The presence of the soldiers who form up around the scaffold as it goes up proves no deterrent.

So strong is local feeling at two of their own being turned off that the City's two Sheriffs, James Townsend and John Sawbridge, are beginning to panic. As Valline and Doyle spend their last lonely moments in their cart, only speculation can recreate the frantic discussion that must have taken place between the City Sheriffs. They have delayed the execution by some two months already, Lord Mayor Beckford having sought royal approval for not holding the hanging at Tyburn as tradition dictated. Now do they dare wait for eleven o'clock, the set time for Doyle and Valline to be hanged? Or should they get it out of the way quickly, before the mob storm the gallows?

The decision is taken to get it done while they still can. Later, the crowd are to lament that 'the Sheriffs hanged the men up like dogs, they would not let them have time to say their prayers'.[2] With the scaffold erected, the cart with the two weavers is drawn up beneath the cross-beam; the nooses are passed over their heads and tightened around their necks. Both men are going to their deaths protesting their innocence. Doyle himself makes one last statement, quoted afterwards in a newspaper:

> *I, John Doyle, do hereby declare, as my last dying words in the presence of my Almighty God, that I am as innocent of the fact I am now to die for as the child unborn. Let my blood lie to that wicked man who has purchased it with gold, and them notorious wretches who swore it falsely away.*[3]

Doyle's references here are specific, and the crowd's anger will be visited later that day on the 'wicked man' whose gold seems to have brought the heavy hand of judgement down on the East End's weavers.

This is a time before the long-drop method of hanging is introduced. The new gallows at Tyburn, erected in 1759, has introduced the moveable platform, but the drop is shallow. At the signal, the platform falls away and the men drop perhaps a few inches, scarcely enough to break their necks, just enough to hurt, and for the nooses to tighten.

And then begins the slow process of strangulation. However determined the victims might be to make a heroic end, they never do. Soon the body's blind need to survive will force them to jerk and to spasm with involuntary panic, twisting in an impossible effort to get air into their burning lungs. The Tyburn jig will last until, with the emptying of their bladders, they find release.

All this time official eyes will have been scanning the crowd as it transforms into an angry mob. How much longer will these men take to die? Can this be finished and the corpses removed before the people storm the scaffold? The soldiers might buy some time, but how much time before they're overwhelmed by the vengeful crowd? No doubt the soldiers are thinking the same; with no time to reload, they would have to rely on bayonets to keep back the angry surge. An uncertain hope. Eventually it is all over, and the two lifeless bodies swing unresisting from the cross-beam. Swiftly they are cut down and bundled into the cart in which they were brought here. Never mind the gallows; that can be left where it is. Just get the bodies away so that the Sheriffs can put some distance between themselves and the dangerous East End.

As soon as the hanging party are gone, the mob surges forward and attacks the scaffold, smashing it to pieces, letting out at last some of the frustrated anger that up until now they've had to keep penned in. Wood flies all over the place, but this is an impotent rage. At one point though, someone has an idea, prompted perhaps by Doyle's curse, 'Let my blood lie to that wicked man who has purchased it with gold'. Soon the mob moves from Bethnal Green and heads westwards to Spitalfields.

One Captain Thomas Taylor is later to testify in court that when he arrived at Spitalfields Market at around five past one, some 4 - 5,000 people were gathered at the premises of the Huguenot master weaver Lewis Chauvet, of 39 Crispin Street. They were crammed 'as thick as they could stand together', and some were in the house destroying it.[4]

Captain Taylor is at the Old Bailey Sessions to testify at the trial of Nathaniel Norris, seemingly the only person to be taken for attacking Chauvet's manufactory. The attack on these premises was not a random act of aggression however. It was, after all, Lewis Chauvet who brought about the hanging of Valline and Doyle by offering the ludicrously tempting reward pot of £500, thereby unsealing the lips of Mary Poor.

Turbulent Times

The eighteenth century was a turbulent time in London, with practitioners of a variety of trades taking action in protest at low pay and long hours. George Rudé points out that a characteristic of eighteenth century London was that 'almost any issue might occasion a riot',[5] and that though many had 'a nationalistic or anti-foreigner façade' they were prompted often by economic issues.[6] But the action was particularly vehement in the 1760s, which Rudé describes as 'the most remarkable decade of industrial disputes of the whole century'.[7] The hanging of Valline and Doyle was not the first execution to be carried out in the East End to try and bring a recalcitrant workforce to heel. In 1768, seven coal-heavers were hanged in Shadwell for the siege of John Green's *Round About* tavern on Old Gravel Lane in protest against the way the call for workers was organised. The threat to order posed by the weavers probably caused the authorities the most concern however, particularly given the trade's reaction to the threat posed by the importation of calico.[8]

Woven from cotton, calico was lighter than wool and cheaper than silk and was hated by weavers of both these textiles; moreover the calico that threatened their livelihoods encased the bodies of many women in London, and this made them a ready target. From 1719 women were being attacked on the streets, their dresses spoiled with ink and even ripped from their backs. Indeed, such was the threat facing the weaving trade that, in May 1765, it even united masters and journeymen in protest, as they marched on Parliament with black flags flying, a symbolic act of mourning, before besieging the London home of the Duke of Bedford for his part in defeating a bill to exclude French silks from the English market.

Parliament had tried to introduce protective legislation, but with limited success. In 1700 the importation of printed calico was banned by Parliament, but not that of plain calico, which could be brought in freely to be printed at the presses established in Lewisham. Parliament resisted calls for an outright ban on calico until, in 1720, a bill was passed by the House of Commons banning the wearing of calico, and indeed its manufacture for soft furnishings. The bill was held up by the House of Lords for some weeks until, in May, the weavers of Whitechapel and Spitalfields gathered in protest. Calico printers were threatened, and women had their calico clothes torn from their bodies. The Lords could not put it off any longer, and the Bill was passed.

Discontent among London's journeyman weavers was given a fresh impetus in 1763 by the conclusion of the Seven Years' War with France and the subsequent resumption of trade across the Channel. French weaving brought to London by the Huguenot refugees in the 1680s had helped make English silk production reach a quality that far outstripped that of the French weavers. However, this quality came at a price. Despite any protective measures the British government might put in place in the eighteenth century, cheaper French silk was being imported, and if necessary smuggled, into the country, undercutting local producers. The quality might not have matched the local product, but price has always had the loudest voice in the market place. London's master weavers, protective of their own profits, would react by cutting the wages they paid to the journeymen who wove the raw silk. This silk was provided by the masters, and woven on looms usually rented from the masters.

The Combinations
But at last the journeymen had had enough, and were coming together in bands called 'combinations' or 'committees' to take the situation into their own hands, a movement known by the general name of the Bold Defiance. Specific and highly detailed rates for work were set by the weavers themselves when they compiled their list of prices, which was ready by August 1762.[9] It specified the rates for each of the many kinds of cloth, and the looms and equipment of masters paying under the agreed rate became the targets for aggression.

Ironically the list set a precedent for the Spitalfields Acts which, while trying to save it, would choke the weaving trade by the time they were repealed in 1824. Indeed, Peter Linebaugh describes the list as 'the social contract' which would be used subsequently by the magistrates when setting the rates of pay for weavers under the provisions of the Acts.[10]

These bands had coded names, like the Defiant Sloop or the Dreadnought Sloop, and just like naval ships they engaged in cutting raids. But unlike the naval tactic of cutting out a ship from a harbour, these cutters would attack the looms bearing the silk provided by master weavers who paid the journeymen badly, or who refused to pay the levy raised (some say extorted) by the combinations. The levy itself has been seen as both a strike fund and as an extortion racket, depending on the point of view.

The combinations were based at specific taverns, and it was an attempt in 1769 to break up the meeting of one of these combinations that brought the Cutters' Riots to a head. The years 1768 and 1769 were particularly turbulent ones, with agitation stirred up among sailors, watermen, coopers, hatters, glass-grinders, sawyers, tailors, coal-heavers and silk-weavers. These disputes were marked by an increase of armed violence: Robert Shoemaker tells that 'the industrial disturbances of 1768-69 marked a substantial escalation in the use of weapons by both protestors and the authorities'.[11]

Cutting
In 1769 the houses and looms of many journeyman weavers were attacked by combinations of cutters, including on 7 August those of Thomas and Mary Poor of Stocking Frame Alley, Shoreditch. It was for their alleged part in this raid that Valline and Doyle were hanged outside the *Salmon and Ball*, and that William Horsford was hanged subsequently at Tyburn.

Lewis Chauvet suffered that August at the hands of the cutters. He had a substantial manufactory at 39 Crispin Street, the end of the street that was demolished in the 1920s to make way for an extension westwards of Spitalfields Market. Here, he made silk handkerchiefs. The premises were raided in August 1769 by a fearsome group of weavers – possibly as many as 1,500 of them – led apparently by John Valline himself.[12] Seventy-six looms were attacked, and Chauvet managed to stop the destruction only by paying out £2 2s on the spot, and promising to pay subscriptions to the Bold Defiance. No wonder that he should be active in seeking the prosecution of the cutters.

Up until then, Thomas and Mary Poor had kept quiet about the cutting raid on 7 August. They may have feared reprisals by the cutters should they inform; indeed, at the trial of Valline and Doyle, Thomas Poor claimed that he had not informed earlier for fear of being shot. However, there is also the suggestion that they may have been hoping someone would buy their silence.[13] Certainly, when Chauvet dangled such a preposterously enticing amount of reward money before the collective noses of the desperate East End weavers, it would be only a matter of time before stories were told.

On 26 September, Mary Poor engaged a friend to write a letter to Chauvet on her behalf, naming John Doyle and John Valline as members of the combination that raided their home. Doyle and Valline were duly arrested, and came to trial at the Old Bailey Sessions (forerunner of the Central Criminal Court) on 18 October 1769. But before this came to pass, matters were brought to a crisis by the raid on the *Dolphin* alehouse on 30 September, which brought the army to Spitalfields.

War on the Combinations
Written demands for subscriptions were sent out to masters and journeymen alike by the combinations. In September 1769, it was decided that the combinations must be broken and the cutting raids brought to an end. Cutting had been declared a capital offence by Parliament in 1765, but this had not deterred the combinations, who struck at night and went disguised. On 30 September, some magistrates (there is uncertainty about how many) went, supported by a file of soldiers, to the *Dolphin* alehouse on New Cock Lane, in western Bethnal Green (now the eastern reach of Redchurch Street: the Victorian public house version of the *Dolphin* is on the corner with Turville Street). As is usual with such sensational events, the details

7

differ from account to account, but the generally accepted version of events is as follows.

The magistrates and soldiers entered the alehouse and passed through the ground floor room where people were drinking contentedly. Among the drinkers were weavers, as would be expected in a Bethnal Green alehouse, and a potboy was going backwards and forwards to serve them. Unsurprisingly, the combination was meeting in the *Dolphin's* upper room, away from the main part of the tavern. The magistrates made their way upstairs. It seems they took the precaution of placing the soldiers in front. After all, the members of the combination would be armed, and though usually this would mean blades, it could also mean firearms.

On reaching the door, the soldiers burst into the room. The combination would have been surprised for a moment, but they reacted promptly and, by all accounts, they opened fire first. One soldier, Adam McCoy, fell dead, having been shot in the head. The rest returned fire, killing one weaver and wounding another; James Briggs was to die later in the London Hospital from infection caused by the bullet lodged in his jaw. Whether a fight ensued is questionable, but at some point, the majority of the weavers managed to escape, possibly across the roofs of the neighbouring houses, as their retreat downstairs would have been cut off. The soldiers managed to reach four weavers and they detained them; a search of the premises found Daniel Murphy, the leader of the combination, hiding in the landlord's bed. He was arrested and brought to trial before the Old Bailey Sessions on 18 October for the death of Adam McCoy, but he was acquitted as no evidence was offered.

After this action, the authorities had no option but to bring in the army, lest violence should escalate in the wake of the raid, and a detachment of soldiers was brought through the City of London – to the irritation of Lord Mayor Beckford – and quartered in Spitalfields. As they were there to protect the interests of the master weavers, the masters were required to quarter the officers in their own homes, as well as contributing to the feeding of the men at the *Three Tuns* tavern. Lewis Chauvet was keen to contribute: the cutting raid at his premises in Crispin Street had unnerved him. He must have been afraid, given that he was prepared to part with the colossal sum of £500 for a discovery about the cutting of his work, at least some of which reward Mary Poor wanted to compensate her and her husband for the disruption of their trade.

The Poors

According to the record of the trial at the Old Bailey Sessions,[14] on the night of Tuesday 8 August 1769, at about a half-past eleven, a group of cutters rapped at the door of Thomas Poor's home, calling out, 'You b[itc]h of a w[hor]e! You son of a w[hor]e! Let us in, or we will cut down your door!' Mary Poor insisted that Thomas stay where he was, as the cutters would treat a woman more mercifully than a man. In her shift, she headed for the door, calling for the cutters to let her put on her petticoat, but they carried on hacking at the door. When she opened it, there was a group of seven cutters who told her, 'Get out, you old w[hor]e; get out of the shop'. They then made their way into the house and headed for the seven looms.

Mary Poor identified only two of the cutters: John Valline and John Doyle. Indeed, she emphasised in court just how much she recognised them. Describing how Doyle had kept her covered with a pistol, she pointed out that he lived only three doors away from her. Also she mentioned that, as she watched Valline destroy silk belonging to Joseph Horton, she asked him, 'You are known in this alley, why do you come here?' That she made no reference to William Horsford as being in the group is curious, in the light of her positive identification of Horsford at his trial two months later.

Thomas Poor could not identify the cutters as they arrived, because he was hiding in the bedroom. As soon as he heard the loom weights begin to hit the ground however, he apparently went to the bedroom door and saw the men by the light of the characteristic large window of the loom room. He identified Valline and Doyle as being among them; like his wife, he made no reference to the presence of William Horsford. He even added the curious detail that the cutters shook hands with his wife on their way out. The Poors' son William testified that

9

Doyle kept his mother covered with a pistol and also with a sword. However, Thomas Riley, one of the Poors' men, was in bed actually in the loom room, and his statements seem to contradict those of his employers.

Hearing the cutters come in, Riley covered himself with his bedclothes, but not before noting that, despite the great weaver's window, he could not make out who the men were in the darkness. He could hear what happened afterwards though. Although he did not know Doyle's voice, he did know the sound of Valline's, and on that night he couldn't recognise any of the men's voices. Riley also testified that Mary Poor did not call anybody by the name of Doyle. The question of visibility is an important one, as the home would not have been lit at that hour. Indeed, Thomas Poor stated that after the cutters had gone, he lit a candle to survey the damage done. In the subsequent trial of William Horsford for complicity in the same raid (which it took the Poors two months to bring to light), there was great attention paid to who could see what on the night in question; but not at this earlier trial.

No alibi statements were given, but Doyle stated that since the raid, and some time prior to the trial, Mary Poor had overheard him once calling her a bitch of a whore; he stated also that he had later taken out a warrant against her. This seems to be borne out by Thomas Poor's statement at the trial of William Horsford that he informed on Doyle and Valline only after Doyle had taken out the warrant for assault, which put his wife into Clerkenwell Bridewell. Doyle swore also that he had never been in the Poors' home.

There were character witnesses; some testified to the general good character of Valline, including one Thomas Foot, who said that Valline himself had had his own goods cut whilst working for him. There were others, however, who gave Valline the character of a rioter. Not surprisingly, one of these was Lewis Chauvet; another was Peter Traquan, a neighbour of Chauvet in Crispin Street. The third was a Mr Dumoissur. The French names of Traquan and Dumoissur suggest that, like Chauvet, they were both Huguenots.

When Valline and Doyle were found guilty and condemned, they were sentenced to be hanged at the usual place. This meant that on the next hanging day they would have been taken by cart from Newgate Gaol to Tyburn, a two-mile journey through the crowds to what was then still a village in Middlesex though already on the northern edge of Hyde Park, with the growing city threatening to swallow it. Tyburn Tree, the famous three-legged, triangular scaffold was still standing.

However, on 9 November, the City's two sheriffs were instructed by the Recorder of London to execute the two 'at the most convenient place near Bethnal Green church'.[15] This was the church of St Matthew, Bethnal Green's original parish church, on the developed western side of the parish. The eastern side, including the Green itself, was still semi-rural and offered much more space for a crowd to gather and witness an execution.

Uncertain as to how legal it would be to amend a judge's decision in this way, the sheriffs referred the matter to John Glyn, the Common Serjeant of London, for his opinion. Glyn was unsure, and instructed the sheriffs to refer the matter to King George himself, which they did on 13 November by applying to Lord Weymouth, the dissolute Secretary of State for the Southern Department. This initiated a correspondence lasting throughout November, which concluded only when the sheriffs received a letter on 6 December giving the king's authority for the change of venue.

After such a delay, no time was wasted: two days later, outside the *Salmon and Ball* tavern (which still stands, though the present Victorian building bears no resemblance to the original 1733 one), John Doyle and John Valline were hanged.

More Hangings
The hanging of Valline and Doyle was not the last hanging connected to the Cutters' Riots. On 6 December, the day the fateful letter arrived authorising the exemplary hanging of Valline and Doyle among their fellow journeymen in Bethnal Green, William Horsford was tried at the Old Bailey Sessions for his complicity in the same raid on 8 August.[16]

Seemingly, the memories of Thomas and Mary Poor had been

refreshed in the intervening two months. This time, Poor identified the seven cutters, whom he named as John Doyle, John Valline, William Horsford, Bill Duff, Andrew Mahoney, Thomas Pickles and Joe Colman, who used the nom de guerre of Jolly Dog. Poor claimed that, although there was no light save that from the window, he could see them as they left, and that he heard Horsford bid Mary Poor goodnight as he, Mahoney and Valline, shook hands with her on their way out.

Mary Poor identified the same men, although she referred to Thomas Pickles as 'Pat' Pickles, and added an eighth name: Mickey More. She claimed that she would have known Horsford in the darkest corner in London, and that she saw him so plainly by the light of the stars and of the moon that she could not have been deceived. However, despite the assertions of Thomas and Mary Poor and their son William, their men stated that it was far too dark to make out anything. Moreover, the Poors' neighbour Abel Downs, who claimed to have been watching the proceedings through a hole in his door, said that it was so dark he could not distinguish one man from another, nor recognise a person's face.

At this hearing, the subject of money was raised. It should be admitted that the Poors were raided twice more after 8 August, after which they moved away from Stocking Frame Alley. They had abandoned the weaving trade, leaving their men in charge of the premises. Mary Poor went to stay with a friend in Limehouse until she was committed to Clerkenwell Bridewell at Doyle's warrant. Thomas Poor had been committed to Tothill Fields Bridewell, but then was supported by charity in the Tower Hamlets.

It is likely that their financial straits may have made them too willing to sell what they knew. Twice during the trial of William Horsford, Mary Poor had to deny charges that she had been demanding money for her silence. Indeed, Thomas Sykes the rent collector testified at Horsford's trial that when he came to collect rent in September, Mary stated that she knew seventeen of the cutters in the combination, and that she would hang them unless they gave her £30.

Thomas Poor admitted that he had informed because of the poverty he suffered; Mary Poor stated that, since the raid, she had applied for money several times to the combination whose members had raided her home. Though she claimed that she decided to inform on Doyle after his warrant put her in prison, Mary also admitted that she had heard of the £500 reward, and that she had asked another woman to write a letter to Chauvet for her. This was two or three days before she was sent to Clerkenwell.

Additionally, Thomas Poor admitted that his wife had applied to a Mr Depont for £170 to secure a public house; also that she had talked to a Mr Traquan, again seemingly for money to secure a public house. Like Chauvet, both names are French, which may be no surprise among Spitalfields' master weavers. That Traquan was a character witness against John Valline in October is suggestive, as is Poor's evasive claim that he did not know what answer Traquan gave his wife; apparently he did not take particular notice.

Unfortunately for Horsford, he advanced what he thought was a watertight alibi, stating that he had been drinking for hours in the *Well and Bucket*, Old Street, with a friend called John Fitzharris and with Francis Barton, a headborough (petty constable) of Shoreditch. Barton testified that they were there drinking until past one in the morning and that, '[a]part from relieving himself, when he was not missing five minutes', Horsford did not leave the pub. The alibi was confirmed by a warrant Barton had just executed before he met Horsford: it was for the committal of a Mrs Gun to Clerkenwell Bridewell.

When the warrant was produced however, the jury noticed that the date had been altered from 5 August to 8 August. The Bridewell confirmed that Elizabeth Gun was indeed committed to its care on 5 August. It seems strange that such a transparent fraud should have been committed. A verdict of guilty was brought in and, on 20 December 1769, William Horsford was hanged at Tyburn, along with two more cutters tried and convicted on the same day. John Carmichael and William Eastman were convicted separately of cutting the silk of, respectively, Robert Cromwell and Daniel Clarke.

A Lynching
The name Daniel Clarke is at the centre of the bloodiest episode of the

Cutters' Riots. By 16 December, despite Carmichael, Eastman and Horsford having been condemned, things had calmed down sufficiently for the soldiers to be withdrawn from Spitalfields. Much to the annoyance of Lord Mayor Beckford, the detachment marched straight through the City with drums rattling and fifes playing, a warlike gesture permitted only to those regiments granted special privilege by the City.

The deployment of soldiers had stung Beckford from the outset, and this latest insult to the City's dignity provoked him to complain immediately to Lord Barrington, Secretary of War, indignantly insisting that the City authorities could deal with any unrest 'without the aid and assistance of a single military man'.[17] However, the exemplary hanging of John Valline and John Doyle seems to have had the desired effect, and order was returning to the East End. Though there was some sporadic activity after December 1769, it was less violent and on a smaller scale; except for the moment when Daniel Clarke walked along Norton Folgate on 16 April 1771.

Although, when most people think of the East End's weaving trade, they think immediately of the Huguenots, there was a considerable presence of Irish weavers in the trade, one of whom was the unfortunate John Doyle. Indeed, there is a good deal of evidence that the Irish weavers of London, and those of Dublin, were collaborating in organised protest. One letter, which was sent from Dublin and addressed 'To the Committee of Silk Weavers in London' was intercepted in the summer of 1768. It includes a reference to 'Dan Clark', who is described as 'an ignorant master' and as the 'cat's paw' of the others. Significantly, he is described as having been '[v]illain enough to swear false'.[18]

On 11 September 1769, Daniel Clarke and his wife were visited by a gang of cutters from the combination based at the *Red Lion Tavern*, presumably that Spitalfields tavern which once was the home of the noted herbalist Nicholas Culpeper. William Eastman was brought to trial at the Old Bailey sessions as being one of the gang. Many witnesses testified in court[19] that after the raid, Clarke had said definitely that he had no idea who the cutters were, yet Clarke himself was very precise with the names of those who had attacked him. Despite this, and the number of character witnesses on his behalf, Eastman was found guilty, and he was hanged on the same day as William Horsford.

On 16 April 1771, Clarke was taking a walk with fellow weaver Benjamin West when they were beset by two men, and then more arrived. Later, in court, West remembered someone calling out something like, 'There goes Clarke, that blood-selling rascal'.[20] Then stones were flung at them. West and Clarke fled. Clarke took refuge in the home of a Mrs Snee in Cock Lane, not far from the *Dolphin* alehouse on New Cock Lane, but soon the house was surrounded by a mob. Clarke made the fatal decision to escape across the garden wall. The mob chased him, and drove him eastwards on to Hare Street (nowadays Cheshire Street), and then into the brickfield on Hare Street Field.[21]

At some point they had stripped him down to his underwear; in the brick field was a pond made by water collected in a pit dug for brick clay. Clarke was thrown into the pond, and then he was pelted with earth, half-bricks and stones for about half an hour. He was rescued from the pond, but then the mob threw him down on a sand hill and started pelting him again, for about a quarter of an hour. He was then thrown back into the pond, and the pelting continued. At one point a stone hit him on the temple, causing him to bleed.

By this time, though Benjamin West said later in court that it was a hot day with some rain, it seems to have started snowing, and soon the snow was too thick to identify the men who assaulted and murdered Clarke. Or so the witnesses said. A man, apparently in a white shirt, was seen pushing Clarke's head under the water; not enough to drown him, just enough to terrify him, but the pelting continued. By the time an official from Whitechapel Prison arrived and Clarke was rescued from the pond, he was half dead. The brickmakers refused to lend their barrow, or even a door, to get him to the London Hospital, or to give him shelter from the snow in their shed. Soon, Daniel Clarke was dead.

Robert Shoemaker describes the treatment of Clarke as one of the rare violent episodes which were 'the exception rather than the norm' during London riots, violence being inflicted usually upon effigies.[22] However, in their treatment of the traitor Clarke, the participants 'imitated the practices of several public punishments': whipping him through the streets, tying a halter around his neck and ducking him in a pond.[23] This may have been an exceptionally violent episode, but it was clearly the weaving community taking its revenge upon Clarke for his part in the hanging of the cutters. When he was accused by the mob of being in league with Chauvet, Clarke was said to have replied, 'Chevat [sic] is worse than me'.

Francis Clarke, a fruiterer and no relation to the victim, testified later at the Old Bailey Sessions that two men of the mob told him that 'they had got Clarke that hanged the cutters'. He stated also that he saw William Horsford's widow Anstis crying. He asked her why she was crying, since she now had 'satisfaction'; she replied that she grieved 'for the loss of my husband and for my fatherless children'. Her friend Judith Morris recalled Anstis calling out, 'Clarke, Clarke, I am left a widow; my child is fatherless on account of you, and more of your companions'. Indeed, Morris spoke of Anstis asking Clarke, 'Do you remember poor William Eastman?' like a vengeful spirit, while the naked Clarke was begging for mercy, and praying to God.

After the lynching, local magistrate David Wilmot advertised for information. Soon he began receiving threatening letters. One, dated 17 April and signed 'One of ten thousand', claimed that 'the fellow we kill'd on Tuesday swore away the life of my dearest friend and if he had had a thousand lives I would with pleasure have taken them'. The letter threatened Wilmot and his family with death within a month and destruction to his home.[24] Another purporting to be from the same author, and dated 21 April, takes more time to explain the injustice of proceeding against 'some unhappy persons who had taken that just revenge which the law would not admit of', exacting vengeance against 'that detestable late object [...] who was thirsting after their blood not thro' any motive of justice but merely for reward'. It is signed 'Fate and the ruler of ten thousand'.

Robert Campbell was convicted of being the man who thrust Clarke's head repeatedly below the water. One Henry Stroud was convicted also of being among the mob pelting Clarke, particularly of throwing half bricks at him after he had been ducked under the water. However, even here it would seem that money influenced the testimonies given against them. Francis Clarke the fruiterer testified that when summonsed to appear in court, the officer who summonsed him offered £80 to be shared between him and one Sarah Scales for their testimony against Robert Campbell. Worse corruption seems to have underpinned the case against Henry Stroud.

Evidence was given that Stroud was one of those who tried to help Daniel Clarke at the end, but a Joseph Chambers, who was caught up by the mob, gave evidence that he saw Henry Stroud pelting Clarke. Chambers admitted, however, that he was encouraged to do so by a gardener called James Knight, who mentioned to him that there was a reward. Indeed, there seems to have been an understanding between Knight and two other men, David Higgins and William Watts, that testifying against Stroud would earn them a £100 reward. Even John Pagett, a constable involved in the case, seemed to have a financial interest: when asked by the court, 'Are you not to have a share of the reward?' his reply was, 'Well, what I have I shall keep'.

The hanging of John Valline and John Doyle on 6 December 1769 provoked great local fury, which may explain why the 20 December hangings of Carmichael, Eastman and Horsford took place at Tyburn rather than among the weaving population. Certainly this is the opinion of Linebaugh, who states that 'the authorities hanged them at Tyburn, not daring to further risk [sic] the ire of Spitalfields crowds'.[25] But the outbreak of violence which resulted in the lynching of Daniel Clarke had to be suppressed with another exemplary execution. Robert Campbell and Henry Stroud, convicted on 3 July 1771 of Clarke's murder, were hanged on 8 July on Hare Street, near the brick field where Clarke was lynched.

By this time however, the violence of the Cutters' Riots, described by Rudé as 'the last, and bloodiest, of the great weavers' outbreaks', had petered out: what activity there was after this was muted by comparison.[26] In a noticeable contrast to the threat of violence attendant on the hanging of Valline and Doyle, the hanging of

Campbell and Stroud 'on a small eminence in the public highway' was carried out 'with a degree of order becoming the solemnity of the occasion', according to a letter from the sheriffs of the City to the 'civil officers' who attended, quoted in the 'Appendix to the Chronicle' of the *Annual Register* for 1771.[27] The *Register* observes that by this time '[t]he infatuation of a deluded people had subsided', and the removal of the bodies to Surgeons' Hall for dissection was conducted routinely.

In the aftermath of the increasing violence of the 1760s, the first of the three Spitalfields Acts was passed in 1773, with subsequent Acts following in 1792 and 1811 to extend the provisions of the original Act respectively to weavers in silk mixed with other fabrics, and to female weavers. The 1773 Act required that the wages paid by master weavers to their journeymen should be set every quarter by the magistrates of Middlesex and the aldermen of the City of London. It also set prices for specific work.[28] Such legislation was meant to bring to a close the disruption in the weaving trade which led to the Cutters' Riots, and the first Act was welcomed as an advance. However, it became clear as time went by that the Acts were strangling the trade they were trying to protect.

Higher wages could not be paid to reward efficiency and innovation, and low wages could not be offered in slack times. Thus the Spitalfields Acts brought periodic unemployment and continual stagnation. By the time they were repealed in 1824, they had virtually killed off the trade, which could not compete with the cloth produced on an industrial scale in the Midlands and the North, or with imported cloth, a point made forcefully by the anonymous author of the 1822 pamphlet *Observations on the Ruinous Tendency of the Spitalfields Act*, who mourns how 'to the great regret of every well-wisher to the prosperity of this country', overseas producers are undercutting London weavers, as are the 'manufactories' outside London.[29]

The author of the *Observations* calls for the removal of restrictions and a greater use of machinery, as well as making use of the colonies to provide cheaper raw materials. However the weaving trade, which had been at the heart of the East End's industrial output, was based essentially on a cottage industry that could not compete with the challenge of manufacturing methods created by the Industrial Revolution. Though weaving would continue in the East End, particularly in Bethnal Green, until the early twentieth century, it would never regain the prominence it enjoyed in the late seventeenth century and throughout most of the eighteenth.

Chapter 2

The Gordon Riots

On 28 June 1780 the Old Bailey Sessions House became very busy indeed. From then until 10 July, eighty-five persons were tried in sixty-seven separate hearings for riots committed between Monday 5 June and Thursday 8 June. Thirty-five of those tried were found guilty. On Monday 10 July proceedings moved across the Thames with another fifty defendants brought before the King's Special Commission at St Margaret's Hill, in the Borough. On Tuesday 11 July, the hangings began.

In 1778 the Papists Act was passed by Parliament, the first of the Relief Acts intended to relax the penalties imposed on Britain's Catholics. However, a number of Catholic leaders were against this new Act. After all, much anti-Catholic legislation went largely unenforced, and their concern was that the new Act would stir up an anti-Catholic reaction. They were right.

On 2 June 1780 rioting broke out in the City of London, the culmination of a stirring up of anti-Catholic feeling by Lord George Gordon, president of the Protestant League. Over the next few days many important buildings were attacked before the violence escalated beyond the City's bounds. Though the Riots were directed initially at the Catholic community, the focus widened to include authority figures and national institutions. Soon the violence degenerated into self-interested looting.

Of the thirty-five rioters found guilty at the Old Bailey, twenty-three were actually hanged. Some of the hangings took place at Tyburn, the principal place of execution for London and Middlesex. There was however an alternative tradition of executing the condemned at the place where the crime had been committed and this was observed now, with hangings taking place in many locations to bring home to Londoners how dangerous it was to break the peace.

Though George Rudé claims that the targets 'were not those living in the densely populated Catholic districts' which included 'the dockside parishes of East London',[1] nonetheless there are three places within the Tower Hamlets which were targeted by rioters on 7 June 1780: Black Wednesday. Two were public houses, and one was the house of a Bethnal Green magistrate called David Wilmot. The arrest of the only person identified as involved with this last assault, however, came after a crisis of conscience in the man who arrested him.[2]

John Gamble

At about six or seven o'clock in the evening of Wednesday 7 June, a mob descends on a large house to the north of Wilmot Square, Bethnal Green Road. The house is the home of David Wilmot, speculative developer and magistrate. James Haburn, a local cabinet-maker, watches what he believes to be about a thousand people start to congregate outside the house. Soon they have broken in, and are beginning to destroy the house from the inside.

The usual method is to enter the place by force, and then to remove and rip out everything combustible and take it outside to burn it on a bonfire. Meanwhile, the belongings of the owner are comprehensively looted. This is referred to as 'pulling down the house', although the house itself was not usually demolished. Thus, as Haburn looks on, every scrap of wood, paper and board Wilmot's house contains is piled bit-by-bit on what will soon be a roaring fire, exhilarating and encouraging the mob in their destructive frenzy.

As well as being a cabinet-maker, Haburn is also a local headborough. Now an obsolete office, the headborough was responsible for enforcing the law locally. Clearly there is no point in engaging a mob of this size however, so he stays where he is for about an hour, or maybe an hour and a half. If he cannot stop the attack on the house, he can at least witness what is happening, and hopefully who is doing it.

21

Haburn has been there some time when he sees someone he recognises: John Gamble, a journeyman cabinet-maker. Being in the same line of work, Haburn has known Gamble for years, and indeed they did work together at one time. Now he sees Gamble coming from the house carrying some boards and other bits of wood on his shoulder. No doubt he balances the materials expertly until he reaches the fire, the glow of which will be all the more visible as dusk begins to fall.

Haburn watches Gamble throw the wood on the fire and then go away toward the house. After three or four minutes he is back with another load, and then another, and yet another. Haburn sees Gamble come to the fire again and again, but doesn't see him enter or leave the house. Then again, this means nothing. There will be a steady stream of people in and out of the house, which is besieged by a huge crowd, so it will not be easy to see who is going in empty-handed and coming out with arms full. Besides, it isn't necessary to go in to get wood for the fire; much of it comes out from the upstairs windows.

Those upstairs won't be dragging things all the way down; instead they throw clothing, furniture, bedding and all sorts from the upper windows. Of course, anything portable and valuable left behind by the owners they will secrete about their persons to sell later. The crowds below will be grabbing gleefully at what has been thrown down, and anything that burns goes over to the bonfire. So, Gamble could have got his wood from wainscoting and furniture being thrown down to the ground below, the fancier pieces no doubt greeted by the whoops of the mob as they smash and splinter.

Haburn isn't the only one to recognise Gamble. Joseph Corderoy, a bedstead maker, sees Gamble go into the house, though he does not see him doing anything else. But Edward Pales, a cooper, sees Gamble on the top of the house chucking the tiles off. He sees other people on top of the house as well, but he does not know who they are. Both men know Gamble and later will testify in court to his being at the besieging of David Wilmot's house.

After about an hour and a half, the impotent Haburn has had enough. The milling crowd will have grown so that by now it will be impossible to glean much useful evidence, so James Haburn decides to make his retreat. As he leaves, the lead is being ripped from the roof and thrown down, along with all the other spoils.

The next day, Haburn happens to step into a public house when whom should he find there but John Gamble. 'John, you're hard at work,' observes Haburn ironically. As a journeyman, if Gamble doesn't work he gets no money, so what is he doing in the pub in the morning? Well, he is bragging for a start. Gamble no doubt sneers as he swears that the mob have done 'Davy'. For some reason though, despite this open bragging, Haburn is reluctant to arrest Gamble. Maybe it is fellow feeling for a former workmate; who can say?

Whatever the reason, Gamble is not taken until the following Wednesday, a week after the attack on Wilmot's house. In fact, it has taken warnings from the watch and from a fellow headborough to get Haburn to do it. It is general knowledge that Haburn knows Gamble, and if he had not taken him, Haburn himself would be in danger of being arrested.

It would seem to have been fellow feeling that stopped Haburn arresting Gamble. A reward had been proclaimed for the arrest of those involved in the destruction, and he admits later in court that he saw the proclamation stuck up, and heard of it. However, he denies that it motivated him to act. He did not claim the reward, and indeed he claims he wishes that there had been no reward placed.

On 5 July, Gamble's case is heard. At this time, trials are decided largely on the basis of witness statements. Gamble does what he can to discredit the witnesses. He asks about what he had on, in hopes that they will say the wrong thing. Indeed he tries to wrong foot Edward Pales, saying that he told the magistrate that Gamble was dressed in a white coat, but Pales replies simply that he did not mention clothing at all. Besides, both Haburn and Corderoy confirm that Gamble was wearing a blue jacket that evening.

Gamble's defence is simply that no-one says they saw him with anything in his hand which might be used to destroy the house. Presumably he sees the wisdom of not denying that he was there. He claims that Haburn told him to 'get out of the way' several days before he took him, which seems to confirm the reluctance to arrest a former workmate. He calls just one single defence witness: John Knight, a cabinet-maker, for whom Gamble has worked as a journeyman for over seven years.

Knight testifies to Gamble's trustworthiness and honesty. Sadly, he also admits that Gamble has a weakness for alcohol which, for Knight, makes him an object of pity, but which may not have the same effect on the jury. He mentions the reward offered for testifying against rioters, and claims that Pales may well have been offered money for his testimony. Perhaps most damaging to Gamble's case though is Knight's answer when asked by the jury whether Gamble was at work at his shop on the day in question. Knight replies, 'He does jobs at home sometimes'.

Unsurprisingly, this defence does not help. John Gamble is found guilty and on 20 July, just over a fortnight later, he is hanged on Bethnal Green Road, facing Wilmot Square. The Square no longer exists; where the entrance once was now sits a Tesco Metro, and the closest we can get to Gamble's view of Wilmot Square is the view of Tesco from the top of Derbyshire Street.

William Hutt

If James Haburn's unwillingness to arrest John Gamble brings a human dilemma to the riot trials, the trial of William Hutt, an apprentice velvet-weaver, reveals how shambolic these proceedings could be. Hutt was indicted for being involved in the destruction, on 7 June, of the dwelling house of a weaver called John Turell on Wheler Street, now Braithwaite Street, Spitalfields. He was taken on the basis of information provided by Henry Myers, a velvet-weaver of Bethnal Green.[3]

When giving evidence, Myers is graphic in his description of Hutt's activity in the garret. Myers saw a bedstead chucked out from the garret window which rested in the guttering, and then he saw Hutt come out and try to throw it over the coping of the building into the street below. He had some difficulty doing this, and when he put his legs over it, Myers thought it would make him fall. But as Hutt threw it over the coping he managed to fling himself back. Meanwhile the bed crashed into the street below. Despite this detail, when asked to comment on the damage caused to the building, Myers is less informative. He states that while he believes part of the house was 'injured', he is not there to say whether the house was destroyed. He is there only to say that he saw Hutt aiding and abetting.

The principal problem with Myers as a witness is his inability to confirm the date. He says that he thinks the house was attacked on the Wednesday, but it might have been on the Monday. He can say it was between one and four in the afternoon, but that's all. Moreover, while he agrees that Hutt was taken up on the basis of his information, when asked how long it was after the fact that he gave that information, he is evasive: 'I would rather you apply to evidence'; when Counsel insists, he replies, 'I do not choose to resolve that'.

There is a world of frustration in the next, and final, remark made to the court by Counsel for the Crown: 'I do not like this witness; as far as I am concerned, as counsel for the crown, I give up the prosecution'. The case falls to the ground, and Hutt is declared not guilty.

Samuel Solomons

On the same day that John Gamble is hanged, another man is hanged in Whitechapel. Tried on the same day as Gamble, Samuel Solomons was found guilty of an assault on Christopher Connor's public house, the *Red Lion*, in Black Lion Yard, Whitechapel. Like Wilmot Square, Black Lion Yard has long since been built over, though it is recalled in the name of Black Lion House which stands on its site. However, unlike the assault on Wilmot's house which saw only one person arrested, three defendants are indicted at the Old Bailey Sessions for the attack on the *Red Lion*, and three more are indicted for theft.

On 7 June, after ten at night, two gangs of rioters come into Black Lion Yard, filling the area outside the *Red Lion*. Among the mob is Samuel Solomons, a pencil-maker who has been supporting his family for about three years since his father died.[4] Christopher Connor has seen Solomons before in Whitechapel and in Petticoat Lane, but does not know him.

According to Connor, Solomons is the third or fourth man to enter the house. Once inside, he begins pulling down boxes as fast as he can. As Solomons goes upstairs, Connor runs after him and sees him, and two or three others, forcing open the chamber door. Connor begs them 'for God's sake' not to tear his place to pieces; by this time they are in the room and Connor's pleas mingle with the sound of splintering wood as the rioters begin breaking open drawers.

Solomons is carrying a bludgeon and a lighted candle; he grabs Connor by the collar as he begs the mob not to spoil his property. Another rioter holds a pistol to Connor's head and growls that if Connor doesn't go downstairs, he will send him down twice as quickly as he came up. Then Connor feels the searing pain of a blow to his arm with something like a small bar, and which feels like it has fractured the bone. He makes his escape downstairs as the assault continues, gets over the fence onto a neighbour's property, and then goes to find his wife. As he does so, he sees the looting taking place.[5]

Specifically, Connor sees Amelia Hall and Jemima Stafford, customers of his who live in the neighbourhood. First he sees Stafford coming out of the house with a bed on her back, which she carries over and puts on the rioters' fire. When she has done this she goes back in. About two or three minutes later she comes out with another bed on her back, and puts this one on the fire as well. Elisabeth Potter, servant to the Connors, also sees this. Stafford then stands by the fire, cheering with the rest of the mob. The presence of women among the rioters is nothing new; indeed Robert Shoemaker points out that the presence of women – and often children too – gave legitimacy to protests: it 'underlined rioters' desires to project the appearance of widespread community support for their actions'.[6]

Connor loses sight of Stafford after this, but a little while afterwards he sees Hall emerging from the house, also with a bed for the fire. His wife Ann sees this too. While the goods on the premises were being destroyed, she jumped out of a low side window to save her life and fell into the street. She keeps clear of the fire because she is afraid the mob will put her in it, until she finds an old cloak and hat belonging to Elisabeth Potter, which she puts on and stands among the mob, hoping they will take her for one of them.

Like Stafford, Hall cheers when the things are put on the fire. Then she goes back inside the house. When she comes out again she has 'a lap full of something'. Christopher Connor can't see what it is though, but his wife Ann sees what she's got: her china bowls, worth half a guinea at least. Later Elisabeth Potter sees Hall in the parlour and asks her if she is not ashamed to see Connor's things destroyed so. But Hall answers that she has as much business being there as any other.

Another looter spotted by Ann Connor is Mary Stratton. Stratton is a lodger of the Connors in a room opposite the *Red Lion*, so when she sees Stratton bring out some things, Connor thinks at first that she is taking them to prevent their being stolen. But when Connor follows Stratton, she sees her give the things to a Mary Pickott, telling her to take them and pawn them the next morning and they will share what they fetch.

After the riot, the thefts of the looters are revealed easily. The morning after the assault Elisabeth Potter goes to visit Jemima Stafford and sees there a bolster, pillow, blanket, and hangings of yellow harrateen (a kind of worsted) which Stafford has stolen from the Connor house; the blanket she recognises as one she was ironing the day before. On the following day, Friday 9 June, Ann Connor goes to Mary Stratton to confront her; she directs her to Mary Pickott, who hasn't given Stratton her half of the money due.

Solomons is not taken until the Sunday after the raid. Christopher Connor goes before Justice Staples to inform against Solomons, who by this time has been taken at the Rotation Office, at the sign of the Angel and Crown, 2-3 Whitechapel Road. He has come there hoping to be admitted as a witness against other rioters, and thus to escape punishment. He is not admitted, however, because he is one of the principal rioters; meanwhile, Connor is able to identify him. Solomons confesses the following Tuesday.

Another person indicted for this riot is one John Barrett, whom Ann Connor accuses of knocking her down and robbing her. Though she is backed up by John Chivers, a shoemaker and thieftaker, Barrett is given his alibi by, among others, Alice Mills. Having got two persons committed to Newgate, she was afraid of retribution since the prisoners had been let out, and went to Barrett for help to move her things.

Barrett is thus found to be not guilty. The third person to be indicted for the assault on the *Red Lion* is one Joseph Growte; however, no evidence is offered against him, with the result that he is also found to be not guilty.[7]

The three thieves are convicted without much difficulty. Amelia Hall states that she was putting her children to bed when she heard of the fire, and that she was never out of her own door that evening. She has called witnesses, but is unsure where they are. Jemima Stafford claims that she stayed the night at Hall's, after a day's haymaking followed by 'a drop of beer'. Both are found guilty of theft and given twelve months each. Stratton says she was framed by Mary Pickott (whose name in the Old Bailey proceedings changes now to Nesbit) out of spite because Stratton refused to let Pickott use her room to have sex with a man. Stratton is also found guilty, and sentenced to six months in prison.

When Samuel Solomons is indicted for riot at the Old Bailey Sessions, his defence is given in the face of Christopher Connor's detailed evidence, supported by a statement from John Clawson, a beadle of Whitechapel parish, who claims he saw Solomons at the head of the mob, carrying a blue flag. Cross examination suggests that Connor only informed against Solomons to get the reward, and that Connor's fear of the mob may have distorted his memory. Connor denies the reward, and retorts that Solomon's holding a candle up between them made it easy to recollect him.

Solomons states that he pawned his clothes on 27 May, so that any evidence of identity is not trustworthy. However, both Connor and Clawson have said that they do not base their identification on the clothes worn by the suspect. Solomons also brings character witnesses, including his employer Henry Lazarus, who testifies that Solomons is supporting his mother and his sisters and brothers, being the family breadwinner since his father died. The defence is not enough either to prove reasonable doubt, or to provoke a recommendation of mercy. Samuel Solomons is found guilty and sentenced to death.

This sentence is carried out on the Whitechapel Road on 20 July 1780, on the same day that John Gamble is hanged in Bethnal Green, just to the north. The following two days will see the execution of ten more prisoners bringing to an end the series of twenty-three hangings in twelve days.

John Lebarty

Among the five persons hanged on the first day of executions were William Macdonald, Charlotte Gardiner and Mary Roberts, all three hanged on Tower Hill for their part in an assault on a house on St Catherine's Lane. Running through the area where a community had been established for centuries, the Lane disappeared with the houses and the people of St Katharine's when the area was cleared in 1826 to allow excavations for the Docks; nowadays its course lies beneath the West Dock.

The victim was an Italian publican called John Lebarty, whose nationality was bound to make him a target for anti-Catholic rioters.[8] As well as a pub, Lebarty owned a slop-shop, where ready-made clothes were sold. It is in the account of this attack that reference is made to the 'associations', which were bands of householders brought together to protect property in the face of rioting. That they were formed by members of the community, rather than by the authorities, shows how the Gordon Riots polarised community attitudes to the rioting. Robert Shoemaker notes that the riots 'caused attitudes towards the mob to harden', and that the forming of the associations caused the rioters to become 'further marginalised'.[9]

Since the previous Monday, John Lebarty has been threatened by Mary Roberts who lived next door to him until, according to him, he got her moved by the parish officers because her behaviour was so 'audacious'. She has been stopping outside his house and shouting out things like, 'You outlandish bouger, I will have your house down!' and, 'You outlandish Papist, I will have your house down!'

Both Lebarty and his neighbours heard this, and so seriously does Lebarty take the possibility of assault on his premises that he lodges a number of his things with Thomas Buddin, who lives opposite. This proves a wise precaution because, on the evening of 7 June, he is forced to flee his establishment when it is attacked by a mob.

The readiness with which the people of the area seem to know how to behave in a riot situation, particularly the need to place lights (usually candles) in the windows, shows how rife rioting had become by the late eighteenth century. Lights placed in the windows showed sympathy with the mob, and prevented assault.

When they see the mob arrive, Elisabeth Jolliffe, who lives across from Lebarty, and Stephen Spackman, a barber in St Catherine's Lane on a visit to his brother-in-law, see to the placing of lights in the windows. Moreover, Spackman closes his brother-in-law's shutters for him as he sees the mob arrive.

Having received a message that the mob were going to burn his property, Lebarty flees his house between ten and eleven o'clock, leaving his servants behind. He takes refuge in the Minories, at the house of one Mr Ewes in John Street, and it takes his servant Elisabeth, and her mother, days to track him down afterwards. Thus he sees nothing of the attack on his pub, nor can he tell who did what. Later, his neighbours give an account in court of what happened on that night, as does Elisabeth Frazer, Lebarty's 14-year-old servant, who was asleep on her bed when the mob broke in.

Her mother Mary is staying the night, and it is she who wakes Elisabeth up. Hearing the noise of the mob, Elisabeth comes downstairs and sees both Mary Roberts and another, a black woman called Charlotte Gardiner, on the premises. As far as Elisabeth can guess, it is past eleven o'clock. She sees that the mob have broken the windows in the tap-room, climbed in and opened the door. As soon as they get in they begin to pull the wainscoting down.

Meanwhile, Elisabeth's mother Mary is being threatened by one Thomas Downs, a runner for one of the local magistrates, Justice Clarke. Forcing her into Lebarty's bedroom, which is next to Elisabeth's, he threatens her with a gun and swears he will blow her heart out unless she tells him where Lebarty's money and papers are. Then someone passes him a sword or cutlass, which Downs pulls from its sheath, and holds over her head, saying he will split her in two if she does not tell him where the money and papers are.

Mary leads the rioters downstairs, but not until they have sacked the bedrooms. Downs says, 'D[am]n you, you old Papist bitch! Come down stairs and show us where the money is'. She shows Downs the bar where Lebarty keeps his liquor and his money. As Downs goes into the bar, she makes her escape.

Lebarty's next-door neighbour Moses Benjamin is a hatter, but he is also a headborough of Aldgate lower precinct. He is at home when the mob comes: and there are a great many of them. Though it is between ten and eleven o'clock, he will not go to bed lest his house is attacked. In fact, he takes his long staff and sets off to find some more peace officers, but finds only four. Later, in court, he testifies that the four peace officers subsequently left him and that he put his long staff indoors.

Stephen Spackman and Elisabeth Jolliffe see the break-in at Lebarty's; shortly beforehand though, Spackman and his brother-in-law see a curious arrival. At about half-past ten, when they were standing in the street within 10 yds of Lebarty's house, they had seen a man with one arm in a sling, coming along the lane with a bottle in his hand, which he proffered to passers-by as he went. He was crying out, 'Popery, popery!', and 'Who will have any of Langdale's gin?' He said he had brought it from the fountain-head; in other words he was one of the many who plundered Langdale's gin distillery on Fetter Lane between nine and ten that evening before it was set on fire. This man is William Macdonald.

Elisabeth Jolliffe is seeing to the lights in the windows when she hears a great number of people cheering. When she opens her door to look out, she sees the mob. There is a man with a flag, one with a bell, and one with a frying-pan and a pair of tongs. Spackman sees the mob as he watches Macdonald join them. They are knocking at Lebarty's door and trying to get in. He cannot distinguish one man from another, but Jolliffe has seen a black woman, identified later as Charlotte Gardiner.

The break-in, as mentioned above, is effected by climbing in through the window and opening the door. After this, the usual procedure begins. While the glass of the bar is broken, the shutters are knocked out and the bar's wainscoting broken, all to the cry of 'Huzza! Down with Popery! Down with Popery!' Jolliffe testifies later to hearing Gardiner cry out, 'Wood for the fire, damn your eyes; wood for the fire!' Similarly, Elisabeth Frazer claims to have heard Gardiner cry out, 'More wood for the fire! Down with it, down with it; more wood for the fire!'

Soon the rioters move upstairs and begin to throw things down through the windows, leading to a continual throwing out of chairs, tables, and bedsteads, such that Spackman believes he sees thirteen or fourteen beds come down. He estimates the mob to number between fifty and sixty. Along with the broken shutters and wainscoting, the rest of the house's combustible contents are taken to make a bonfire some 50 or 60 yds away, on Tower Hill.

While this is going on, William Macdonald seems keen to spread the violence. Shortly after he is seen helping to get a bed out of a window, Spackman sees him leave the house and go down the street a little, to a china shop where a Thomas Morris is staying. Macdonald calls out for the keys. Morris, who is visiting from Deptford, comes to the window and calls down that he hasn't got the keys; he adds that the family are all out, and that he will defend the door. Not to be thwarted, Macdonald calls out that Morris is a Roman Catholic, and that his house will come down.

At this, a cry breaks out: does Morris have a Bible in the house? Spackman asks him to show his Bible to the crowd to satisfy them. But then someone calls out that he believes Morris to be a true Protestant, and that the house should not come down. Macdonald tries once more, retorting that Morris is a Roman Catholic despite what anyone says, and that the house should come down, but it seems no-one is prepared to follow this up. Macdonald then goes back to Lebarty's house, before going next door to the house of Thomas Brummage, where he knocks with a poker or iron bar and calls for candles. A woman in the house flings some candles out of the window at him; he picks them up and carries them into Lebarty's house. (Thomas Brummage may be the Thomas Brumett who appears as a witness at the trial of Mary Roberts and Charlotte Gardiner – see below.)

Among those collecting the things thrown down from the windows is Mary Roberts, who was so vocal when threatening Lebarty earlier in the week. At one point, Roberts is seen to drag a bed out, helped by another rioter: they cut it open and toss the feathers about before dragging it to the end of the lane. Thomas Brumett, a milkman who lives two doors away and has known her for many years, sees Roberts passing his house again and again, carrying away Lebarty's beds, pillows, and bolsters. He does not note how many parcels she takes but, to the best of his knowledge, she is with the mob all night.

In the meantime, Charlotte Gardiner is egging on the rioters. Another neighbour, Letitia Harris, was not there when the mob first came, but she arrives not long afterwards, and at about twelve o'clock she sees 'the black girl' carry a bed out of the house on her shoulders. Later she claims to have seen Gardiner bringing things out some thirty or forty times in all. She also hears her cry out to someone, 'D[am]n you, you bouger; why don't you work away? The fire will be out; more wood for the fire!' More things are thrown out, and she carries them away to be burned.

Having escaped from the house earlier, Elisabeth Frazer returns sometime between twelve and one o'clock, to see if she can save a few of her own things. As she goes in, the bar itself is being pulled down by the mob; among them is Mary Roberts. They pull down a great deal of the brickwork, which is witnessed also by Spackman. Frazer also sees Charlotte Gardiner in the house, very busy and cheering to the mob. When Frazer approaches her, Gardiner is bringing two candlesticks out of the dining-room. She calls out to the mob, 'Huzza, my boys; well done! Down, down with it!'

By this time, Spackman believes that Macdonald has gone, but Elisabeth Jolliffe sees him, between two and three in the morning, a lighted candle in his hand, pulling down the wainscoting of the one-pair-of-stairs room and throwing it, and the chairs and furniture, out of the window, crying, 'Down with Popery!' There are three or four other men in the room who bring things for him to throw out of the window. Jolliffe has never seen Macdonald before, but she sees his left arm in a sling and hears someone call out to him, 'Well done, soldier; though you are lame, you work very well'.

The sacking of Lebarty's property continues through the night. Thomas Morris, having made his escape earlier on, returns as daylight is coming in. It is at this point that the gentlemen of the householders' association come. Morris sees Roberts in the window of Lebarty's bedroom, and advises one of the association men to aim his gun at her in order to intimidate her. The young man does so. Roberts, who is leaning out of the window and seems very drunk, tells him he might 'fire and be buggered'.

Some days later, Moses Benjamin, the headborough, arrests a man called George Turner, a neighbour of his and someone he has known 'some little time'.[10] On the night of the riot, having gone to a house opposite Lebarty's, Benjamin saw Turner and his wife active in the destruction of the property. He saw Turner steal a shirt or shift, which he picked up and put in his pocket, and then, between two and three o'clock in the morning, he saw Turner take a grate out of the house. Turner acknowledges that he took the grate, and his wife takes Benjamin to the house where she sold it. Benjamin even has the man who bought it up before the magistrate; he says his man broke it up and made nails of it.

When the case comes to trial however, Turner is found not guilty. His defence is that he was on duty as a watchman at that time. He was ordered on the watch at nine o'clock, and did not come home till five in the morning. He adds that he was stationed half a mile from the place where the sacking occurred.

What is most striking about Turner's trial though is Lebarty's attitude when giving evidence in court. He seems overcome by lassitude. After going over what Benjamin told him, he admits that he does not know what a great many people told him. He claims also that he does not want to punish Turner now: 'let God Almighty overtake him another time'. When asked whether he knew that Turner was a watchman in the parish, he replies that he does not know. This attitude is noticeable when he gives evidence at the trials of other rioters. Lebarty seems to have accepted his fate as a victim.

During the trial of William Macdonald, Lebarty describes his pub and slop-shop the day after the riot as 'like a ship that is cast away upon a rock. The doors, windows, wainscoting, the bar, and everything, were all torn to pieces'. He becomes even more fraught during the trial of Mary Roberts and Charlotte Gardiner. He describes how Roberts 'terrified' him, and how, in her threats, she 'was like wild fire to burn the world down'. There is almost a fatalistic tone in his voice as he describes how she 'fulfilled her word; my house was destroyed that night', and how he saw her at his window the following morning: 'She had taken possession of the house; she was leaning out at the window; she had the command of the house'.

This lassitude is displayed most clearly at the trial of Thomas Downs. Downs, whom Mary Frazer accuses of threatening her with gun and sword, had been in Lebarty's house in the early evening of 7 June, when he asked for change of half a guinea. When some days later, Lebarty goes with Mary and Elisabeth Frazer to the Rotation Office in Whitechapel to give evidence against Downs, Lebarty has a seeming change of heart and tells Mary Frazer that he does not want to give evidence, that he will have nothing to do with it. Being a stranger in the country, he decides not to stir up trouble. In court, he says he is unable to remember on what day they went to the office: 'I was so disturbed in my mind I cannot recollect'. When asked why he did not think of arming himself against the mob, he replies, 'What could I do? They were all against me.'

Unlike that of Turner, the prosecutions of Macdonald, Gardiner, Roberts and Downs are supported by ample witnesses for the prosecution. William Macdonald claims that for the past six months he has been suffering 'an affliction' which is so painful that he has to hold out his other hand in front of him as he walks, lest anyone should touch his bad arm: 'for if anything touches it, it goes to my heart'. He claims also that while being held in Clerkenwell Bridewell, he has not been able to send to his regiment for a character reference. Still, he is found guilty and sentenced to death.

Mary Roberts claims that she felt herself under threat from the mob, who asked her whether she was a Catholic and threatened to smother her if she did not throw the things into the fire. Indeed, she claims that somebody threw a bolster over her head and almost smothered her. She brings her sister-in-law, also called Mary Roberts, to testify to her 'exceeding good character', and to point out that she is a widow with one child. Another neighbour of Lebarty, Thomas Buddin, with whom Lebarty lodged some of his things ahead of the riot, testifies that Mary Roberts was actually rescuing papers for Lebarty. Nevertheless she is found guilty and sentenced to death, as is Charlotte Gardiner, for whom no defence is recorded.

Downs incidentally is found not guilty, despite the detailed evidence proffered by Mary Frazer. On the Monday she goes with Elisabeth to Justice Clarke's office, but is prevented from going in by a guard of soldiers, who have been brought from the Victualling Office to East Smithfield to take away some prisoners. It may well be his connection with Justice Clarke which saves Downs. He provides an alibi that he was in another pub called *The Ship* with a different group of people from around nine until late in the evening. From the Old Bailey Proceedings, which are not full verbatim accounts, there seem to be contradictions in the statements of these witnesses. They seem to say that he left with John Wilkinson, another runner, around ten o'clock, while saying also that he left around midnight or half past with Sarah Hart, with whom he lives.

Downs is fortunate enough, however, to have a defence counsel, which at this time is still rare. Counsel tries to confuse Elisabeth and Mary Frazer, and the Proceedings give quite extensive lists (for them) of questions and answers put to these two witnesses. The fatalistic Lebarty, being the last witness called, may perhaps have undermined the prosecution case. Downs himself says nothing in his defence except: 'I leave my defence to my counsel and my witnesses'. Such confidence may have relied on his connection with Justice Clarke, and it was certainly not misplaced.

William Brown

On Tuesday 11 July, William Macdonald, Mary Roberts and Charlotte Gardiner were hanged on Tower Hill, an old-established place of execution associated with the beheading of illustrious persons such as Thomas More and Thomas Cromwell. As has been mentioned, on this first day of the hangings, a total of five persons were hanged for riot. As well as Macdonald, Gardiner and Roberts, William Brown was hanged on Bishopsgate Street, and William Pateman on Coleman Street.

William Brown's story is one of the most poignant to come out of the aftermath of the Gordon Riots. On the first day of the hearings, he was indicted for assaulting the home of Carter Daking, a cheesemonger living on Broad Street; for putting him 'in bodily fear and danger of his life, and stealing from his person one shilling.'[11]

At about two o'clock in the afternoon, Carter Daking is in the counting house of his premises on Bishopsgate Street. Through the window, which looks out into the warehouse, he sees two men who come through the warehouse and up to the window. When Daking asks what they have come for, Brown, with his hat in his hand, says, 'Damn your eyes and limbs: put a shilling into my hat, or by God I have a party that can destroy your house.'

This is the day after Black Wednesday, the day London erupted in violence and properties were destroyed all over the place. Daking saw this violence, and that no soldiers had arrived to help; he has every reason to believe this day will bring more of the same. In the moments it takes Daking to reflect on this, he becomes aware that the man facing him is holding a clasp knife. It is not a big knife, but it is a knife. The second man, taller and more slender than Brown, stands silent as Brown threatens Daking that if he does not give over a shilling, Brown will bring his men and take the house down.

Daking decides on prudence, and puts a shilling in Brown's outstretched hat. With this, the two men turn and leave the warehouse. Daking's man Thomas Baldwin follows them, no doubt at a discreet distance, and sees them cross over to the oil shop. Here they make the same threat. It is some ten minutes later that William Brown is taken.

In court, Brown's defence is essentially that he was too drunk to know what he was doing. He calls a witness, a victualler called Thomas Smith, 'who will prove I was so much in liquor that I did not know what I was about'. There is more of a reason for this than is immediately apparent: Smith testifies that he has known Brown since the latter went aboard the HMS *Serapis*, built across the Thames in Rotherhithe and launched just over a year previously, in March 1779. He explains that Brown served aboard her at the battle of Flamborough Head in September 1779, a hard-fought battle between the British ship, under Captain Richard Pearson, and the USS *Bonhomme Richard*, commanded by Captain John Paul Jones.

Though the *Serapis* and her consort vessel, the privateer *Countess of Scarborough*, were forced to surrender after the *Bonhomme Richard* was joined by the firepower of the USS *Alliance*, they achieved their goal of protecting a Baltic-bound convoy of some fifty sails. Brown explains that he was wounded in this engagement with the Americans, and that as a consequence, he loses his senses when he has had a little drink. He pleads nevertheless that he has done a great deal of good to the nation, and begs that the judge will save his life and let him serve again.

After leaving the *Serapis*, Brown did have another berth until four months previously, since when he has lived with his brother on Wheler Street. He has no means of support, but he was paid three guineas' bounty money either on the day in question or the day before. Brown was in Smith's house that day, and was 'fuddled' when he left around eleven or twelve o'clock. Smith did not see him again after that. That bounty of three guineas may well have been the cause of his drinking, and of his being convicted of robbery.

Though mercy was shown at many of the court hearings which followed the Gordon Riots, none was shown to William Brown. The London jury convicted him of robbery, and Mr Justice Nares condemned him to death. He was hanged on Bishopsgate Street on 11 July 1780. Perhaps he was unfortunate in that his case was heard on the first day of hearings at the Old Bailey Sessions.

THE GORDON RIOTS

The Gordon Riots were unlike previous riots, and did not have the popular support enjoyed by earlier uprisings. In a real sense they meant the end of 'traditional' rioting in London; instead they were the expression of a new, violent kind of riot, which threatened the community rather than roused it. As Robert Shoemaker points out, 'Attitudes towards the mob would never be the same again'.[12]

Chapter 3

Highway Robbery

The execution in 1783 of John Austin closed a chapter in England's punitive history. The small Middlesex village of Tyburn, named after the river that flowed past it, was traditionally one of London's places of public execution. In 1571, it became London's principle place of execution with the erection of the feared Tyburn Tree, the great triangular gallows whose shape is recognisable in so many representations from the period.

But by the 1780s London was changing, and the rebuilding of Newgate Gaol prompted the decision that executions should be carried out there, dispensing with the need for the hanging day procession to Tyburn. From December 1783 until May 1868 a gallows was erected on hanging days against the wall of the gaol, and accordingly the street was widened at the top to accommodate the crowds gathering to watch the condemned swing.

When John Austin, highway robber of Bethnal Green, was hanged on Friday 7 November 1783, he thus earned the dubious distinction of being the last person to be executed at Tyburn.

John Austin
In the last quarter of the eighteenth century, trade blossomed in London. The Thames was beginning to fill up with merchant shipping to such an extent that the riverside development of wharves and quays was beginning to stretch downriver, heading for Limehouse and swallowing up the smaller shipyards. Soon the river would become blocked with shipping. This increase in trade was beginning to draw people to London in the hope of making a better life for themselves. One such hopeful was John Spicer, a poor labouring man from Grays in Essex.[1]

On Tuesday 21 October 1783, John Spicer wraps his possessions in a bundle and leaves Grays, heading to London to find work. As the day wears on, he finds himself in Ilford, which is not actually on the road between Grays and London. Perhaps he hitched a lift with a carter heading for Ilford rather than walk the entire way.

At Ilford, Spicer makes for the *Coach and Horses*, its name announcing it to be a coaching inn. He will be taking care of his finances until he can establish himself, and a coach seat to London would cost a shilling, a lot of money for someone in his position. Maybe, though, he can afford an outside seat on the roof, where impecunious travellers grasp their clothes about them as the wind whips at every loose extremity, and they clutch both their belongings and the rail as the coach jolts its way along rutted country roads and teeters around tight corners. Or perhaps he will walk.

It is at the *Coach and Horses* that Tuesday evening that Spicer meets John Austin, and they agree to travel into London together the next day. It is possible that they walk to London because they do not arrive until Thursday, and it seems unlikely that a coach would take over a day to travel from Ilford to London. Spicer and Austin lodge together on Tuesday and Wednesday nights, during which time Austin takes the opportunity to find out why Spicer is going to London, and what little he has on him.

On Thursday 23 October they reach Whitechapel which, in the 1780s, was on the edge of developed London. Just to the east is the great open ground of Mile End Waste, streaked with substantial pathways but with only occasional strips of buildings. In the east is the solid, fifteenth-century bulk of the Church of St Dunstan and All Saints.

Austin takes Spicer along the bustling Whitechapel Road to the *White Swan* on the south side. It is about nine o'clock in the morning. Having settled Spicer, Austin tells him to wait there, and not to stir. He is going to find proper lodgings for them both, and will bring back something for breakfast. Of course, Austin has no ready money, and he persuades Spicer to part with a guinea, on the promise that he will bring back the change along with the victuals.

It is not until some three or four hours later that a man by the name of Patrick Bowman approaches Spicer. He begins by apologising on Austin's behalf for the delay and for his not coming back himself. The truth is that Austin has managed to secure lodgings, and has sent his old friend to guide Spicer to him. They head eastwards until they reach the *Blade Bone* public house near the Mile End turnpike, where they meet up with Austin – but this is not where they are staying. Maybe after 'one for the road' all three set out together, heading northwards to the lodgings Austin has found.

After a while, at about six o'clock in the evening, Spicer is beginning to wonder why they are in the middle of a field, beside a ditch; they are a way from the road, and all he can see is the lights of some distant lamps. Bowman stops; they won't be able to get over the ditch easily so he leads Spicer to the corner of the field, while Austin stays back to relieve himself.

'This is a very comical place to look after a lodging', comments Spicer; and as he does so, Bowman turns, drawing a cutlass from under his smock. What light there is catches the blade as he tells Spicer to hand over all he has, or he will cut him down. Presumably he is relying on the countryman being weakened and confused, but he has reckoned wrongly. Rather than being afraid, Spicer runs at him and grabs hold of him. It is down to Bowman to react now, and he slashes with his cutlass, aiming blows at Spicer, cutting him across both hands. Blood flows as Bowman slices at Spicer's wrist, his head and his leg. Despite this, Spicer is not going to give in, and he fights back hard.

As he resists, Austin comes up to the two men. Hoping he is coming to help, Spicer calls out to him, wondering why he does nothing. But Austin grabs Spicer by the neckerchief with one hand, and by the leg with the other, and throws him down on his back. As Spicer slams down on the ground, maybe struggling for wind after such an unexpected fall, a cord is produced and his hands are tied. Austin and Bowman then fall upon him and rob him of his possessions.

This is not, however, as quiet a place as Austin and Bowman appear to have thought, and all this exertion has been overheard by a gardener called James Strong. In the dim light, Strong rushes over to help the prone victim. Maybe Spicer saw Strong coming because he calls out to the evening sky, 'For the Lord's sake, come and help me!' Strong calls back as he runs over; Austin and Bowman stop immediately, get to their feet and run away.

Rushing past the prone victim, Strong runs after the fleeing thieves in order to take them, but they stop and brandish their weapons as a warning: Bowman shows his cutlass, and in the growing darkness Strong mistakes Austin's stick for another cutlass, so he retreats and returns to Spicer. It is too dark for Strong to see enough of the men to recognise them again.

Spicer is in a terrible condition, with blood all over him. Rather than wasting time trying to untie him, Strong lifts up the weary Spicer and takes him back to the house of his master, Giles Wells, who is just coming in as Strong brings in what Wells will describe in court as 'the most deplorable figure [...] that ever was seen'.

Wells does everything he can to stop Spicer's bleeding wounds and to comfort him, though without hopes of his recovery, and sends Spicer off to the hospital. But Spicer is a resilient man. He survives, and will see at least one of his attackers up before the Old Bailey Sessions on a charge of highway robbery, for which the punishment is death.

Early the next morning, Strong is out in the fields seeing whether the robbers may have dropped something which can be restored to Spicer. After all, so poor a man cannot sustain such a loss. As he trudges through the field, Strong sees Spicer's hat still lying where he was attacked, and within moments he sees something else: John Austin is coming across the field toward the hat, his clothes stained with blood, and looking at the ground as he comes. True it was too dark for Strong to see enough of Austin and Bowman to be able to recognise them again, but he cannot miss the stains of John Spicer's all too freely flowing blood smeared over Austin's clothes.

Strong approaches him and asks what he is looking for. Clearly Austin did not see Strong properly either last night as he replies he is looking for some lost money. Within moments, however, Strong has reached Austin and overpowered him. Austin is clearly no match for the man who could carry Spicer's limp body across the fields, and soon Austin is locked up in Giles Wells' stables. Austin protests his innocence through the stable door, but later at the watch house he confesses to the assault and robbery. He directs the enquiry to the *Blade Bone*, but no clue can be gleaned there as to where Bowman might be found.

Meanwhile, Wells is trying to find any incriminating evidence Austin may have hidden in the stable. He sets a man to clean out the stable and, while he watches him work, the man puts his hand in among some straw, and pulls out a silk handkerchief and a pair of stockings. They belong to John Spicer. When Austin is shown to him later, Spicer is able to make a positive identification.

The case comes up before the Old Bailey Sessions on Wednesday 29 October, five days after Austin was taken, and concludes on the Saturday. Austin is charged with violent theft, and Spicer's handkerchief and stockings are advanced as evidence. Austin's defence is that he met Bowman for the first time on the night in question and knew nothing of the intended robbery. The enquiries of a constable called Yardley, however, prove that Bowman and Austin have known, each other for some time.

Without hesitation, he jury find him guilty. After consulting with his fellow judges on the Bench, the Recorder James Adair says that the case is such that he should pass sentence of death immediately. When Austin is asked whether he has anything to say about why sentence of death should not be pronounced against him, he replies, 'I don't fear death, as I am not guilty, and shall die innocent'.

Adair then addresses Austin, telling him that he has been 'convicted by the verdict of a very merciful Jury upon the clearest and most satisfactory evidence of a crime so atrocious as to demand the most severe and immediate interposition of justice'. Not only, he says, is the king determined to stamp out highway robbery, of which this is so clear an example, but Adair finds it particularly cruel that Austin preyed on one whom he had seduced into expecting he would receive kindness at his hands. It is Saturday; Adair will prepare his report and submit it to the king on Monday to ratify the time of execution, but he warns Austin to prepare for 'speedy and exemplary justice'.

On the morning of Friday 7 November 1783, six days after his conviction at the Old Bailey Sessions, John Austin is taken by cart in the usual way from Newgate to Tyburn. On the way he behaves with great composure, and no doubt the usual crowd jostles for the sight of the last person to be hanged at Tyburn, making the most of the very last chance to see the old procession. Many a prisoner has gone bravely – or at least with a crowd-pleasing show of bravado – to a gruesome end at Tyburn. No doubt the crowd expects John Austin, highway robber, to damn the sermonising of the Ordinary, the chaplain to Newgate Gaol, and to launch himself bravely into the unknown. If so, they are to be disappointed.

As the noose is placed around his neck, Austin begins to tremble so that the whole gallows starts to shake violently. After the Ordinary retires from the cart, Austin addresses the crowd, but this is no dashing farewell:

> 'Good people, I request your prayers for the salvation of my departing soul. Let my example teach you to shun the bad ways I have followed. Keep good company, and mind the word of God'.

The cap is then drawn over his face, and he raises his bound hands, crying out, 'Lord, have mercy on me! Jesus, look down with pity on me! Christ, have mercy on my poor soul!'[2]

As he calls out this imprecation, the cart is driven away and he falls, but the noose has slipped round to the back of his neck and it takes Austin fully ten minutes to strangle slowly to death. Perhaps the mob finds some meagre entertainment in the sight of his desperate writhings, the traditional Tyburn Jig, but after he is dead some of the disgruntled mob tussle for, and gain possession of, Austin's remains. Seemingly put out by his tame end, they carry the body back to Newgate, dropping it there to be buried.

Thus, with a whimper, ends the tradition of processing the condemned from Newgate to Tyburn.

George White

The robbery of John Spicer was not a typical highway robbery, involving as it did the selection and cultivation of a victim, or 'mark', who is then duped into coming to a secluded place and assaulted. The more usual form of highway robbery was to cruise the roads for travellers and to take a chance on the terror you inspire as you ask them to stand and deliver. Highway robbery made the country's highways unsafe, and its travellers vulnerable; it was the coming of the railways that finally made for safer travel.

The field where Bowman and Austin attacked John Spicer cannot be identified, but it was one of many such open spaces in the northern parts of the Tower Hamlets, far from the congestion of riverside development. Cambridge Heath, to the north of Bethnal Green, provided the robber with travellers heading east and west, as did Old Ford Lane (now Road), the ancient highway to the equally ancient settlement on the River Lea. A particularly comic moment happened on this road between two and three o'clock in the afternoon of 10 July 1740, when a surgeon called William Martin was faced down by an armed man while travelling from Bonner's Hall in Bethnal Green to Old Ford.[3]

When Martin handed over his money to George White, former soldier, who was not mounted, White was not convinced that Martin had delivered everything he had; nor did he believe Martin's assertions that he had no watch. Martin was in fact playing for time, and hiding his watch as best he could, because there were people working in the fields some forty or fifty yards away. But White lost his temper and pulled his trigger.

The powder in the pan fizzled and went out. Though the pistol was loaded, it would seem that the touch-hole was plugged. At this, Martin jumped down from his chaise and, brandishing his long whip, chased White along the road. After some thirty yards, White turned to brazen it out with his now useless pistol, but Martin picked up a handy half-brick and flung it at White, who made off again. Eventually, Martin caught up with White, and was belabouring him with his whip when a mounted man arrived and helped him take White to a magistrate.

Richardson and Conway
To attempt a theft in the middle of the afternoon, near a field being worked by labourers, shows how opportunistic the highway robber could be. However, the practice of London's highway robbers was changing; more were starting to take their chances on the streets of the more developed parts of London. George Rudé has noted already that, as early as 1731, highwaymen 'were brazenly moving in to the centre' of London from its outskirts.[4] There was more chance of a prize on the busy urban streets, if also more chance of detection.

Though Rudé focuses on the western side of London, his point holds true also for the southern areas of the Tower Hamlets, which, from the sixteenth century, developed along with the age of exploration in England and the growth of the City's maritime trade. No open highways here; rather the robbers preyed on those whose business took them through the tightly packed streets, lanes and alleys which framed the great Mile End Waste.

The life of the highway robber was forced on many by poverty and need, but there are many instances of robbers who turn to the trade because they are unable to cope with a run-of-the-mill life of respectability. The temptation of such an uncertain life of adventure attracted chancers who were unprepared for what they were doing. A classic example is the attempted robbery in May 1770 by Michael Richardson and Peter Conway, two men in their early twenties. Though a grim story, it shows also how badly thought through such robberies could be.

This was not Peter Conway's first criminal venture.[5] On 6 July 1768, at the age of 18 (or maybe 19), he was convicted of stealing ducks and sentenced, with his fellow thief Thomas Cruise, to be whipped. More seriously, on 17 January 1770, he stood indicted as co-defendant on two of three charges of highway robbery. The first was that on 22 December 1769, Conway, John Chapman, William Paterson, and John

Milbank attacked and robbed Thomas Brewer, a surgeon and apothecary living at Mile End.

The robbery took place between seven and eight in the evening, as Brewer was walking along the New Road, a thoroughfare running through what was then open ground, to the west of the London Hospital. About halfway along the road he was attacked by a gang of men, but it was too dark for him to confirm later whether there were four or five men. He remembered that they told him to say nothing to anybody about the attack, and to have pity on the poor weavers; the latter no doubt was a blind.

All four were acquitted, but then the second charge was put, that on 21 December, the day before the attack on Brewer, Conway, Chapman and Paterson attacked and robbed John Chambers, the master of Ratcliff workhouse. He was attacked near the *World's End* pub by St Dunstan's Church, at about a quarter to eleven at night, as he was walking home from Ratcliff Cross via White Horse Street (now Road). He had a lantern in his hand, by means of which he was able to see the face of one of his attackers. Later, he identified Paterson as the man he saw.

Conway and Chapman were acquitted, but Paterson was convicted and sentenced to death. Paterson was also sentenced to death, as was Chapman, for a highway robbery on a John China at between five and six in the evening on Boxing Day 1769. Like Brewer, China was attacked on the New Road.

Acquitted on both charges, it appears, nevertheless, that Peter Conway developed a taste for highway robbery, since in the spring of 1770 he tried his hand at being gang leader, with three accomplices. Just over six months after his last appearance there, Conway was back before the Old Bailey Sessions on another charge of highway robbery. However, this time the robbery had a far more serious outcome than those committed in Stepney in the previous December.[6]

It is around eight o'clock in the evening on Saturday 26 May 1770, and shoemaker Robert Dunn is in his shop in Princes Square, near Ratcliff Highway. Established only in the 1720s as the focus for

London's Swedish community, in competition with their Danish-Norwegian neighbours in Wellclose Square, Princes Square is more modest, but still impressive. One Richard Joyce is in the shop too, and is able to testify later that four men come into the shop looking for guns. This sounds curious, but Dunn's brother is a gunsmith; he lives at the same address, and so keeps his stock in the same shop. This stock comprises not just guns, but also edged weapons. The four men are Michael Richardson, Peter Conway, William Jackson and Owen Fox.

The first into the shop is Jackson, who asks whether Dunn has any second hand pistols for sale. As his brother is not there, Dunn serves them, producing two horse pistols. Though not a pair, they are decent brass-mounted items, and more than serviceable. Eight shillings is the asking price for the two. Conway seems to be the leader of the gang, because he brings out some coins to pay, but has only a shilling piece and some halfpennies. No doubt with a sigh, Jackson produces a half-guinea piece and hands it over. Dunn gives him two shilling pieces and then has to count out twelve halfpennies to give him the remaining sixpence.

Leaving Princes Square they make for the nearby house of Daniel Thomas, who fences for them. He lives behind the *Two Children in the Wood* pub, near the ducking pond. Only Mrs Thomas is in, and Jackson goes in to hide the pistols behind a picture that hangs behind the door. As the pub is conveniently close, the gang then make for that. During the course of their evening's drinking they try to persuade an acquaintance, Thomas Blackston, to come robbing with them. He is out of work, after all, and could perhaps do with a little something to defray expenses. Blackston refuses to get involved.

On the following evening, after a day trip to Peckham and some pretty solid drinking, the gang ends up at Wellclose Square around half past five. They make for the *Two Children in the Wood* and, while Conway, Richardson and Fox stay in the pub, Jackson goes to retrieve the pistols. It is only now that they notice they have a problem. They may have two pistols, but they have no bullets. After spending some time trying to work out what they can do, Richardson and Conway come up with the idea of cutting up a pewter spoon and using the pieces as slugs.

As soon as they have done this they stow their pistols under their coats and set off; Conway and Richardson are leading, the other two following at a short distance. After all, they don't want to appear to be a gang. They make their way towards Stepney and as they draw near yet another pub, *The Crown*, what transpires to be a footman approaches them. *The Crown* stands in front of some houses by the side of the ditch: presumably the Black Ditch, a now lost waterway which rose in Shoreditch and cranked its way through Bethnal Green before dog-legging through Stepney and heading for Limehouse.

The footman is John Kilpack, servant to a Mr Glanville of Redman's Row, Stepney. Conway, his pistol concealed beneath his coat, goes up to challenge him, but a glance prevents him saying anything. From his appearance Kilpack clearly has no money, so the gang pass on, letting him go on his way unharmed.

About 20 yds further on, by a row of houses near a cross post erected to prevent the cattle going through, they see two clearly prosperous men coming towards them. It is close to ten in the evening – in fact, the watchman cries ten three or four minutes later – but it is not very dark, and the two men are wearing light coloured clothes. One is a butcher called William Venables, the other is his neighbour, a carpenter called Rogers. They come from Whitechapel, and are returning after a walk out to Stepney.

Conway tells the gang, 'I'll stop these men', and pulls out his pistol. Jackson, though, says he wants no part of this; that the men are too strong for them to deal with; and he walks off. He is within 12 yds of what happens next.

Richardson pulls out his pistol; Conway stops the walkers with his gun, demanding they hand over their money, while Richardson backs him up. Fox is right behind them. But Venables, the stouter of the two, is a robust man and not prepared to put up with this. Maybe he senses something hesitant about these young men. Whatever prompts him to do so, Venables brings his cane swiftly and heavily down on Richardson, knocking him to the ground, and then he does the same to Fox. As they are getting up, once again he knocks them to the ground.

What is Conway to do? Should he threaten Venables with his pistol, or will that leave him vulnerable to Rogers? After all, he only has one shot. But then everything happens very quickly. As Richardson picks himself up for the second time, he opens fire at Venables. Conway can do only one thing, and he shoots Rogers. Both men are killed on the spot. Venables drops to the ground; Rogers falls against the wall in front of the houses. Rogers has been shot through the head, Venables in the throat.

The gang are now panicking. They have at their feet the dead bodies of two men they have shot down in front of a row of houses from which at any moment people will start to rush. So, shall they take time to search the bodies for booty? Without risking a moment they make a run for it, rushing off towards Stepney. Fox has a hat in his hand, which he has taken from one of the bodies, but as they pass the *Dolphin*, about a quarter of a mile from St Dunstan's Church, he throws it clear, not wanting to be found with an incriminating item on his person.

Eventually they reach Shadwell, where they go into an alehouse below Cock Hill, at Stone Stairs, and have a glass of gin each at the bar. They don't stay there long however; maybe the encounter has enlivened them, or maybe having been thwarted they want some return for their evening. Whatever the reason, they are soon out of the pub and heading south towards the river, ending up in Wapping, where they rob a man of his watch and eighteen shillings below Execution Dock.

They then make for the City and another public house, in Dark House Lane by Billingsgate Fish Market. They stay there overnight, sleeping two to a bed, and on the following morning they pawn the watch they stole in Wapping for thirty shillings.

Meanwhile, the bodies of Venables and Rogers have been examined by a surgeon, Mr Callop, before the coroner's inquest takes place. Venables has a very large shot wound on the right side of his neck, stained black with the powder which still gives off its distinctive smell.

The wound on the left side of Rogers' forehead speaks of a shot straight into his brain. Both men must have died immediately.

It takes only two days for things to unravel. On the Wednesday, William Jackson is taken on suspicion of his involvement in the attack. Offered immunity and a reward of £100, he begins to name names and is admitted as a witness for the Crown. On the next day, Conway calls alone at the *Blue Ball* on Chamber's Street, Goodman's Fields, to see Thomas Buckman, who is presumably a fence. Buckman, however, has seen the advertisement offering a reward for the arrest of Conway and Richardson and wants the reward. But, believing Conway to be armed, Buckman goes out into the Minories to get help.

While he is gone, Conway heads to the 'necessary house'; when he returns to the tap room, Buckman arrests him. Buckman searches him, but finds no firearms. He also braces himself to search the toilet, but it is too deep to find anything. Conway is bundled into a coach to take him to the Bow Street office of the magistrate Sir John Fielding. As the coach pulls away, Conway calls out, protesting his innocence: 'I could not shoot two men myself'.

Richardson is taken the following Wednesday, 7 June, in the upstairs room at his father's house in Well Street, near Mile End New Town. Richardson claims he was not involved, that he was standing relieving himself against a nearby house while the attack happened.

Nearly a fortnight later, while Richardson and Conway are in Newgate Gaol awaiting trial, one David Thomas visits an acquaintance there called Smith. David is the father of the fence Daniel Thomas in whose house Jackson hid the pistols. Thomas recognises Richardson, but has never seen Conway before. Later in court he will claim that Conway confessed to him that he was one of the killers, but that Jackson was the other, rather than Richardson.

On Wednesday 11 July, Peter Conway and Michael Richardson are brought up before the Old Bailey Sessions on a charge of murder. In court, Richardson claims that it was Jackson who shot Venables, and Conway accuses Jackson of giving evidence to get the £100 reward and free pardon. Both base their defence on stout denial. Richardson puts forward some character witnesses; Conway claims that he has sent down to Gravesend for his witnesses, but that they have not yet come. Both Conway and Richardson are found guilty, and sentenced to death.

They receive sentence immediately: they are to be executed on the following Thursday, and their bodies are to be hung up in chains as a warning to others. Accordingly, on Thursday 19 July, Peter Conway and Michael Richardson are hanged at Tyburn. After their execution their bodies are cut down and taken eastwards through the City and out to Bow Common, an open space between Stepney and Bromley.

Here their bodies are put in chains and then swung up into the air on a gibbet. It is most likely that they are caged to keep the bodies upright for as long as possible, and to prevent grasping hands from grabbing body parts; given the special powers imputed to hanged bodies, the parts would be much prized. The bodies prove a huge attraction. The estimated attendance over the next five days is more than 50,000 people; on the Sunday, the place is like a crowded fair, giving many people the chance to make proper money by selling food and drink to the sightseers.[7]

Branch and Descent

Apart from the amateurish nature of some highway robbery, the image of the highwayman is tarnished further by accounts of sickening violence meted out, a link between eighteenth century highway robbery and present-day mugging. The romanticised image of the legendary Dick Turpin, who himself spent time in Whitechapel, conceals much brutality. A gruesome example of unnecessary violence is found in the case of Randolph Branch and William Descent, who were indicted in 1752 for highway robbery, and for the murder of their victim, Joseph Brown.

The real name of 29-year-old William Descent was William Dustings.[8] Having served at sea, he fell into a dissolute lifestyle in London when presented with his share of prize money from his service aboard the *Medway* as a midshipman. It was when he came in to

53

Plymouth at the end of his service in May 1751 that he met with the 15-year-old Branch, who was finishing his time aboard the *Ruby*, having been sent to sea by his family in a vain attempt to get him out of criminal ways. The two formed a friendship which was later to prompt Descent to seek out Branch in London.

Though far younger than Descent, Randolph Branch had an extensive experience of crime.[9] In 1750, at 14 years of age, he was named as one of a gang involved in the burglary of a widow, and later in the robbery of a brandy shop. The first time he appears as a highway robber is on 5 June 1752, when he helped William Signal and William Ward waylay one George Derby at the end of Bridges Square on the Ratcliff Highway between eleven o'clock and midnight.

The only weapon they had was William Signal's pen-knife, which he held to Derby's throat as the others robbed him. Tried on 25 June, Signal and Ward were found guilty and sentenced to death; Branch was not tried, having been admitted as an evidence, i.e. granted immunity in exchange for his information.

Neither Branch nor Descent are so fortunate when, later that year, each tries to get himself admitted as an evidence against the other for the brutal assault on Joseph Brown. This is a particularly brutal case. Though violence was not unknown in the pursuit of highway robbery, it was usually a means to an end: to overcome resistance and force the victim to yield booty, or else to help the robber get away. As Robert Shoemaker points out, violence committed in the course of a street robbery 'usually had to be committed expeditiously'.[10] But the beating inflicted on Joseph Brown kept his attackers on the scene unnecessarily.[11]

At about ten o'clock in the evening on Sunday 9 August 1752, a man called Joseph Williams is standing at his front door on Wiltshire Lane, near Virginia Street, Shadwell. In the darkness, he makes out what looks like someone he knows lying on the ground. When Williams goes over, he sees it is Joseph Brown, brew-house clerk and an acquaintance of his. He begins to lift him up, but Brown is covered with blood: later, Williams will describe how handling Brown's bloodied body 'made me as bloody as if I had dipped my hands in a pail of blood'. Brown is still alive, so Williams rushes some ten yards to the *King's Head* inn, where Brown is living, to summon help.

Mrs Lowrey, the landlady of the *King's Head*, helps Williams get Brown to the inn, and they send for a surgeon, Robert Pell, who arrives at about eleven o'clock. When he examines Brown he finds he is still bleeding, his head and face very much bruised and swollen. Pell does what he can: he manages to stop the bleeding, dresses the wounds, and promises to come back the next day.

Earlier that day, about five in the afternoon, Elizabeth Hall and Alice Dormer were at the house of Mrs Anne Stitchbourne on Rag Fair (now Royal Mint Street) when Randolph Branch and William Descent entered. Elizabeth and Alice may well have been prostitutes; the lady of the house was a fence.[12] Alice was lying with her head on the table, and Mrs Stitchbourne was in bed. The men went into her room and asked if she would buy anything they could steal. She said she would; if she didn't have the money she could get it from a neighbour.

Some five or six hours later they came back with a nice silver watch. Sent to bring beer, Alice got back to hear the men ask thirty shillings for it, and to hear Mrs Stitchbourne offer them twenty-five. When dealing with a fence it's rarely a seller's market, and they agreed. They were staying the night, so there was no problem with Mrs Stitchbourne paying them in the morning.

With Descent carrying a heavy stick, the pair left Rag Fair, and went to the *Prince Frederick's Head* in Rag Fair for a drink with a Walter Roberts. When the three left together, they met a man whom either Branch or Descent knocked down and robbed of three pence and a knife. They then went to an alehouse on Ratcliff Highway where Roberts left them. Later, between nine and ten o'clock, Branch and Descent left the alehouse, presumably in hopes of better success. As they passed the end of Virginia Street they saw another man not far away.

At this point the accounts diverge; understandably, when making their statements later, each blamed the other for the assault. Whoever wielded it though, Joseph Brown was clubbed down with Descent's heavy stick. Unlike the previous victim, however, when Brown was on the ground his assailant continued to beat him about the head; the thud of heavy wood on bone and the grim sounds of the skull cracking must have sounded all the clearer in the empty night. So badly was he beaten that a splinter was chipped from the knob on the end of the stick. When the beating finally stopped, Branch dipped into Brown's pockets and helped himself to the watch and money he found there.

When Descent and Branch had all they thought there was to take, they left Joseph Brown bleeding and headed towards Wellclose Square, where they saw yet another potential victim, Edward Holt. Branch stopped and challenged him; when Holt tried to strike out with his cane, Descent knocked him down. This time though the two were thwarted. Attacking someone violently in a residential square is not a good idea, and people were beginning to come to their doors and out into the street. Branch and Descent made a run for it without stopping to rob Holt.

The next morning, after sharing the proceeds, Branch goes back to bed at Rag Fair, while Descent and a friend called Joseph Crane leave for Deptford. On the way they call on Walter Roberts at the *Prince Frederick's Head*, arriving between eight and nine o'clock. While they are there, word comes that a robbery has been committed near Wellclose Square, and that the victim has been beaten so badly that he is not likely to live.

By the time Descent reaches the shipyards of Deptford, three thief-takers have arrested Branch, who is still in bed when they call and who is quick to implicate Anne Stitchbourne for fencing the watch. In fact, later that year she will be convicted of receiving and transported to a penal colony in America.[13] With Branch secured, the thief takers go to Deptford to find and take Descent.

From the moment each is taken, they both ask to be made an evidence. When each is examined individually before the magistrate, Justice Manwaring will not allow him to be admitted as an evidence, but adds that he may speak without incriminating himself. Descent is examined first, and claims that Branch was the culprit, while he reproached the younger man for what he was doing. If Branch had wanted money he could have asked Descent for some, instead of robbing others. When Branch is examined, he of course blames Descent for attacking people while Branch reprimanded him.

When, on 14 September, Randolph Branch and William Descent are indicted for highway robbery, Walter Roberts does not confirm which of the two attacked the first man after leaving the *Prince Frederick's Head*, though he witnessed the attack. However, he is less cautious when describing his meeting with Descent the following morning. Roberts tells how 'the next morning after he had knocked down the brewer's clerk' Descent showed him his stick, and the place where a splinter had come out on impact.

Roberts claims also that Descent admitted that he beat Brown over the head, and took a watch and some silver from him. Moreover Joseph Crane, who went to Deptford with Descent, states that as they went along, Descent showed him the stick and said, 'It was I that did that job in Wellclose Square last night'. When asked what he understood by 'that job', Crane replies that he understood it to be 'what the man said in the alehouse of abusing a man'.

Both Descent and Branch put forward alibis that are not believed; they are convicted and sentenced to death. Both are then indicted again, though this time for murder.

It is the ferocity of the attack on Joseph Brown which is the distinctive aspect of this case. John Spicer was wounded grievously when attacked by Patrick Bowman, but this was as a result of his fighting back. Similarly, Venables and Rogers were gunned down after Venables attacked Richardson and Fox. But Joseph Brown was beaten savagely while he was down. Just how savagely comes out in the murder trial, which immediately follows the trial for robbery.

During the trial for highway robbery, there were hints as to how badly Brown was injured. Now Robert Pell tells how he brought in another surgeon, Mr Harrison of London Hospital, and how the first thing they saw on examining Brown's head on the Monday was part of his brains lying on the hair, just above the temple on the left side.

When Pell separated the scalp from the skull and peeled it back, they saw a skull more fractured than Pell had ever seen. A splinter of bone he believed to have been driven two inches into the brain, and they had to leave one bone fragment in place, for fear the whole brain would come out if they removed it.

Every day after this, Pell was obliged to remove more pieces of the shattered skull that were pressing onto the brain. On the third day, Pell found that a large piece of bone was loose, the fracture running down Brown's forehead. He removed the bone, and in a few hours Brown recovered his senses. Up until now he had been lying as if in a stupor. Sadly, Brown could remember nothing of what had been done to him at the time of the robbery.

After a while, the danger of Brown's brains becoming released by the removal of bone fragments became so great that Pell had to stop. Brown remained critical and, on 31 August, he died. After his death, Pell opened him up in Harrison's presence to gauge just how much damage had been done. He found that most of the bones of the skull had been fractured, and the left hemisphere of the brain he describes later as 'absolutely dissolved by a mortification'. There is no doubt that the injuries he received caused his death.

The impression on the jury as they hear of Pell peeling down Brown's scalp while he was still alive, removing splinters of bone, the brain threatening at any moment to collapse with the removal of one bone fragment too many, can only be imagined. Not surprisingly, Branch and Descent are found guilty of murder, and again sentenced to death. They receive sentence immediately. It is Wednesday 20 September; they will be executed on Friday 22 September, and under the provision of the Murder Act of 1751 their hanged bodies will be delivered to Surgeons' Hall to be dissected and anatomised.

Highway robbery peters out in the nineteenth century because of the increased use of the railways, making travel safer than the days of stagecoaches, but it was already on the wane when John Austin was taken to Tyburn to acquire his dubious distinction of being the last person hanged there. Rudé notes that though crime as a whole rose during the Peninsular Wars, later in the eighteenth century, it was the result of 'a rising tide of 'economic' crimes or crimes against property', whereas 'the more violent types of crimes – armed robberies, murders and hold-ups – were on the wane'.[14] The highwayman was becoming a thing of the past and, like most things of the past, would over time acquire a romance at odds with the incompetence and the violent realities of the majority of such thefts.

Just as the fields of Bethnal Green, in which John Spicer was attacked, and the open fields along Old Ford Road have long since disappeared, so have most of the East End's traditional open spaces. Bow Common, where the bodies of Conway and Richardson were hung up for view, has long since surrendered to development, surviving largely in the name Bow Common Lane.

Likewise, both Wellclose Square and Princes Square have been lost to development, both having been demolished comprehensively in 1968, thus destroying two of the most architecturally important areas of the Tower Hamlets. Wellclose Square has some of its street plan extant, though the only building that predates 1968 is the St Paul's Church School. Princes Square has also disappeared; the only reminder of its existence is a memorial to the church that once stood at its centre and contained the bones of eminent Swedes Daniel Solander and Emmanuel Swedenborg.

The robberies committed to the south of the Tower Hamlets give an insight into what the area along the riverside was like before the coming of the docks. London Docks, the main dock of which opened in 1805, was to wipe out many of the small lanes in the area of Shadwell and Wapping, though much of it was built on previously open ground. Warehouses would soon spread out from the docks, and Wiltshire Lane, where Joseph Williams saw the prostrate Joseph Brown, has long since disappeared. What remains of Virginia Street, where Brown was spotted by his attackers, is lined with former warehouses.

Chapter 4

The Reverend Russen

By 1777 the fearsome triangular gallows known as Tyburn Tree no longer stands in the Middlesex village of Tyburn, having been dismantled eighteen years before. A moveable gallows occupies its place instead, but still the nooses dangle, waiting for throats to choke.

It is around this gallows that, on 12 December 1777, an expectant crowd waits while two men pray vehemently, making their peace while they have the chance. Some of the men in the crowd have removed their hats and stand slightly ashamed, after one of the men on the platform has interrupted his prayers to tell them off. This grim place should be as sacred as a church. His face is stern with the indignation of deep-felt injustice, and he resumes his prayer for the welfare of the wife and children he will leave behind.

There is a moment of silence while the nooses are placed around the necks of the two condemned men who stand on the platform, their arms bound. When the platform falls away, the victims drop a few inches, and the miserable process of strangulation begins. Thus ignominiously ends the life of the Reverend Benjamin Russen, master of the parochial charity school of the church of St Matthew, Bethnal Green. If his end is ignominious, the reason is all the more sordid.

Ann Mayne
When the Parish of St Matthew, Bethnal Green, became a reality in 1743, after decades of argument and counter-argument, it had one school for the children of the poor, Parmiter's Foundation, founded in 1722. This had taken quite some time to arrange, the will of London

silk merchant Thomas Parmiter having been proved forty years previously. Parmiter had left money to found a school for the education of ten poor boys from the locality, but by the time the new parish church was finally consecrated in 1746, it was teaching thirty.

The church initiated a voluntary subscription to create a second school for the children of the poor and, in 1763, the parochial charity school opened, taking in thirty girls. Two years later, ten boys were added, with the condition that all pupils be clothed as well as educated by the school fund. The presence of a school full of young girls seems to have proved rather too tempting to the Reverend Russen who, in 1777 finds himself in the Old Bailey Sessions court facing multiple charges of rape.[1]

On 18 June 1777, Mrs Russen is lying in; soon the voluminous issue of the Russens will be augmented once again. The Reverend Russen is downstairs with one of his daughters after their midday dinner. One of the pupils, 9-year-old Ann Mayne, is helping out. Though a warm day, Russen is sitting by the kitchen fire; apparently he is feeling sleepy, no doubt because of the warmth. Eventually his daughter rises. She has to go upstairs to mind the girl pupils, her duty since Mrs Russen's confinement, and Russen hands her his watch so that she might keep time during the lessons, noting that it is twenty-five to two. He'll be up by two to take care of the boys.

His daughter no doubt calls to Ann to come up to lessons, but Russen stops her. 'No, let her stay to watch me. I don't want to fall in the fire if I fall asleep.' After all, he'll be upstairs by two. Ann can come up with him and slip into her lesson. Resignedly his daughter climbs the stairs to the schoolroom, right above the kitchen, leaving her father sitting with drooping eyelids, and Ann Mayne trying to think of something to do to keep her occupied. Surely the last thing she wants to do is to sit watching this old man doze by the fire? It's a warm day, and perhaps the heat of the fire causes her mind to wander, but then she hears her name and looks round.

'Ann. Come over here.' Russen's voice is no doubt gentle. After all, she's done nothing wrong. She gets up and walks over to him. 'Right here, Ann.' She stands beside him, waiting. But then he takes her in his lap. Why? Maybe he's just being friendly. She sits there for a moment, but then thankfully he puts her off again. It must be getting towards two, so he'll be getting ready to go upstairs to the boys. But he holds on to her still, and then despite the almost oppressive heat of the room, she feels very cold. Having raised her petticoats the Reverend Russen begins to touch her; after a moment, he unbuttons his breeches.

Soon her ordeal is over. He gives Ann a red and white handkerchief to wipe herself dry. The colours remain vivid in her memory, and she will recall them readily some months later in the witness box.

'I wouldn't think of telling anybody about this, Ann.' His face will have taken on a menace she has never seen before. 'If you dare tell anyone – your mother, your sister – I'll flog you like you've never known.' This threat will prove effective though, and she will keep the secret until it is brought out into the open by circumstances.

'Look at this kitchen, Ann. It needs tidying. See to it.'

As he says this, his daughter comes down. 'Father, it is nearly two.' Perhaps she was expecting to see him dozing in his chair, and is surprised to see him on his feet. Could he not sleep? He could not. She calls to Ann to leave her tidying and come up to class, but Russen answers her, telling her that Ann must miss her lesson. His wife is indisposed, so someone has to do the housework. Once again his daughter resigns herself to her father's whims and goes back upstairs; he follows her, having composed himself properly.

The following month it is Ann's tenth birthday. Maybe the family celebrate her birthday in whatever way they can afford, particularly as over the past month her parents have been beating her 'unmercifully' (as their landlady Mary Pearce will testify) for playing truant, not knowing why she wanted to avoid contact with Benjamin Russen. Perhaps they have a joint celebration for Ann and her sister Mary, who turned 15 in the same month. It is 18 July, a month to the day since Ann's ordeal.

Later Ann will testify in court that she had difficulty passing water for four or five days after the rape, but there is no recorded exploration of her psychological state in the prosaic, selective records of the *Proceedings*, just the state of her bodily functions. Being a trial for rape, the law at the time required only that specific physical criteria be met. It does not consider anybody's state of mind. It is nearly two months before Russen abuses her again.

On Thursday 11 September, around five o'clock in the afternoon, the Reverend Russen is out in the schoolhouse's garden with three of the boys from the school, having returned from a dinner engagement. Because of the dinner, being unable – or unwilling – to teach the boys that afternoon, Russen has given them a half-holiday. The girls are less fortunate; Mrs Russen is on her feet now, so she is looking after them in their schoolroom. She doesn't state whether or not Ann Mayne is with the other girls – and if not, why not – but Ann is in the vicinity when Russen sends the boys across to the church to ask for horse manure for the garden. In these times before internal combustion, those vehicles not pushed or pulled by people are drawn by horses or ponies, so manure is in good supply.

When the boys are safely out of the way, Russen calls Ann Mayne to him and takes her into the Committee Room – like the kitchen, it is on the ground floor, below the schoolrooms. Again he puts her on a chair and has his way with her. Her ordeal is protracted; Russen thinks her hears someone approach, and rushes to the door, but there is no-one there. This time, she will testify, it doesn't hurt as much as the previous time; though it does still hurt and she tells him so.

On Friday 19 September, Ann's sister Mary is sorting through the washing. Since their mother has to work, their landlady Mary Pearce obliges occasionally by washing the girls' shifts. As Mary has Ann's shift in her hands she notices that it feels stiff, 'like buckram' as she is later to describe it in court; buckram being a stiffened cotton or linen fabric. Examining it more closely, she sees what she will describe as 'some yellow stuff' which is causing the stiffness. She goes to Ann and asks her what it is, no doubt unprepared for Ann's account of the way Russen has treated her. He has been Mary's schoolmaster too, and surely she will never have thought of him as treating one of his girls in this way.

Mary tells Mrs Pearce about the deposit and what it means. Mrs Pearce did notice a similar deposit the previous June when washing the shifts, but thought Ann perhaps had a sore of some kind. Mrs Pearce then sends to Mrs Mayne, and when she arrives back from work she is told everything that has happened. There is no record of what she says – seemingly she is not asked this at the trial – but the following morning she takes Ann to see a doctor, one Mr Gilson of Whitechapel, who offers a free surgery in the mornings for the local poor. Gilson examines Ann and sees that there is a slight inflammation, but he makes no particular note of her case. He will be more careful later when asked to examine more girls from the same school.

The next thing Ann Mayne knows is that her mother is taking her to another man, David Wilmot, the local magistrate. The complaint is made; Wilmot collects a neighbour called Hawkins, a trustee of the school, and the two head for the schoolhouse to collect Russen and bring him back to Wilmot's house. A doctor has been called in, and at Russen's request a second doctor is sent for, one Haines, who was treating Russen earlier in the year. Ann is examined by the doctors and the inflammation is clear. Haines asks the other doctor to internally examine Ann, but quickly tells him to stop as it causes her intolerable pain. One thing they can assert after their examination however is that her hymen, the protective membrane ruptured during penetrative intercourse, is intact.

Clearly there is a case to answer, and the following Tuesday Russen is summoned before a panel of magistrates: Justice Wilmot, Justice Spiller, Justice Durden and Justice Bosworth. He is heard and allowed to leave, unmolested. According to Russen's own account in court – which is not challenged – it is decided that there is no capital charge to be made. However, his being taken up has brought Ann Mayne's charges to people's notice, and it emerges that she is not the only girl claiming to have been raped by Benjamin Russen.

More Victims
On 19 March, Sarah Hawkins becomes 10 years old; shortly before this (her mother cannot remember when), she approaches her mother, telling her that she is sore. Mary Hawkins does not examine her, but

gives her some Fuller's Earth ointment to apply to get rid of the soreness. She claims afterwards that she assumed the girl had overheated herself with running. After it becomes known what Benjamin Russen did to Ann Mayne however, Mary remembers what Sarah said and takes her to Mr Gilson's free surgery. This is Tuesday 30 September, but there is still evidence of inflammation. However, as with Ann Mayne, the hymen is still intact. Sarah is to testify in court that Russen raped her regularly every Tuesday morning from 21 January to 18 March inclusive, the day before her tenth birthday.

Sarah states that on the morning of 21 January she was there at six o'clock on Russen's instructions, in order to light the schoolhouse fire. He took her upstairs to the lobby of the boys' classroom, lay her on 'a bed', unbuttoned his breeches and penetrated her. The boys arrived at seven, so he had to be reasonably quick; according to Sarah, he took a quarter of an hour. He did the same the following Tuesday morning, and for the subsequent seven Tuesday mornings, leading her up the first steps, then going behind her and following her up. As with Ann Mayne, Russen threatened Sarah that she would be hurt if she told her mother anything.

A third girl comes forward. Like Sarah Hawkins, Rachael Davis has heard what has happened to Russen, and she goes to her mother 'in a sad fright' with a curious question: what is sodomy? She has heard that Russen has been taken up for sodomy, and wants to know what the charge might mean. Her mother tries to understand what she means, and finally Rachael says that 'if it is for meddling with the girls, I am afraid it is true'. Hearing this, her mother presses her to explain what she is saying: Rachael tells her everything.

As well as being master at the charity school in Bethnal Green, Russen was an assistant preacher at the Lock Chapel (presumably the chapel in Kingsland, to the north-west of Hackney). He would take Rachael up to the chapel with him. On Friday 20 June, however, as they were coming back in the coach, he asked 'whether I would let him have my maiden-head'. The baldness of the statement gives no idea of context, coming as it does from the proceedings of the Old Bailey Sessions Court, and it seems a curiously bold move. Still, this is two days after his first rape of Ann Mayne, which may explain his boldness. And Rachael was 15 years old, at a time when the age of consent was still 12.

Unsurprisingly, Rachael refused, at which he pulled up her petticoats and raped her. She tried to stop him, and struggled to get free, but he forced her. Once again, he did not withdraw until he was satisfied, and he wiped Rachael down afterwards with his handkerchief. Examined at her mother's insistence by Gilson at his free surgery on 2 October, Rachael exhibits signs that violence has been administered. There is evidence of laceration, and her hymen is broken.

She claims later that he threatened her he would punish her if she took away his character, and added that 'there was no harm in it as he was a minister'. Her mother's surprise at the news that Russen had been taken up was because she had always considered him to be 'a worthy man', and no doubt this helps account for Rachael's silence. Moreover, in court her mother testifies that while she is an honest child, 'she is rather babyish of her age'.

On 15 October 1777, nearly a fortnight after Gilson's examination of Rachael Davis, the Reverend Benjamin Russen is up before the Old Bailey Sessions on multiple charges of rape. He is arraigned before a bench which includes Sir William Henry Ashhurst KC and Sir James Eyre, Baron of the Court of Exchequer, who take the lead in his trial.

The courtroom had been rebuilt some three years previously and reflects changes in legal practice, particularly the presence of a semi-circular mahogany table where counsel for prosecution and defence can sit. Until the later decades of the eighteenth century, lawyers participated little in court cases, the basis of a trial being the confrontation of defendant by plaintiff before a bench of judges, and the jury participated much more than is customary nowadays. By the time Russen is brought to trial the presence of counsel is established, but there is no reporting of their questions in the court proceedings. Russen's defence counsel appears only in his appeal to the Bench to allow points to be put, and in the Bench's comments.

At Russen's request, each plaintiff – or prosecutrix, to be exact –

puts her case separately. First Ann Mayne is brought in. Both she and Sarah Hawkins, when they come to give evidence, are asked carefully before their prosecutions begin whether they understand fully what it is to swear an oath, and where liars go after they die. This is not just a courtesy but a legal requirement of any girl to be sworn in a rape case. Still, Justice Ashhurst takes a moment to reassure her: 'Don't be afraid, so long as you speak the truth you need not be afraid of anybody'. Again, as she gets to the main part of her evidence, he encourages her: 'Speak out, and don't be afraid'. Given that she is only 10 and is accusing her schoolmaster, a respected member of the community, this may be easier said than done.

Still, Ann does speak out, and her words testify to how frightened and confused she is. The nature of the *Proceedings of the Old Bailey*, whereby a selected account of the trial is given rather than a verbatim record, adds somewhat to this confusion. Russen is charged with raping Ann Mayne on 18 June and 11 September 1777, but from some of the evidence she gives it seems that he is being accused of raping her in the January as well. This may arise from confusion with the case brought by Sarah Hawkins, who appears both as Mary and Sarah Hawkins. Her mother is called Mary. Moreover, the fourth charge brought against Russen is that of raping 'Mary Hawkins the younger, spinster' on 25 March. Despite the confusion, however, it is the nature of the evidence brought which matters.

The evidence of the deposit on Ann Mayne's shift is significant, but it is the evidence given by the doctors as to the state of the girls' bodies which is crucial. As noted above, no evidence is recorded concerning the psychological impact of the rape on the victims; this was not an issue in the legislation of the time. Evidence is given by the doctor, Haines, as to the tenderness of Ann Mayne's inflamed groin on examination and the intolerable pain produced by a gentle internal examination carried out quite soon after her being raped. But this evidence is merely confirmatory. What is far more significant is the question of the hymen.

While the charge of the rape of Sarah Hawkins is being heard, two doctors – Gilson and the curiously named Hyman – testify concerning her hymen. Both doctors confirm that an intact membrane means that no intercourse has taken place, but Gilson makes a significant remark. Asked by the Bench, 'Do you mean that there could be no degree of penetration without the Hymen being broke?' he replies, 'Very trifling'. Asked to clarify by Baron Eyre ('But do you say that there could be no penetration at all without the Hymen being broke?'), he replies, 'not into the body'. Rachael Davis by contrast has a broken hymen, and there are signs of violence.

Given the medical statements, the Bench could have ruled that there was no evidence of penetration in the cases of Mayne and Hawkins. However, Justice Ashhurst decides not to do so. The matter is referred to the jury and, despite the evidence that her hymen was unbroken and that thus there was little likelihood of penetration, a verdict of guilty is returned against Russen for the rape of Ann Mayne. He is found not guilty on the other charges, but this is little consolation: Benjamin Russen is sentenced to death.

Some two months after receiving sentence, the Reverend Benjamin Russen says farewell to his family for the last time and is taken out from the darkness of Newgate Gaol into the crisp December air. Stepping from the doorway he is surrounded by a crowd, straining to see the faces of the condemned. Will they look afraid, or brave? As the crowd jostle, above their heads rings out a cry: 'Stand clear! Look to yourselves! I am the first hypocrite in Sion!'[2] Benjamin Russen strides through them to the mourning coach which waits him, in company with the Reverend Mr Hughes, the Ordinary of Newgate, an officer of the Corporation of London standing in for the Sheriff, and an undertaker, who within a few hours will be taking care of Russen's remains.

Legal Implications
It is the conviction of Benjamin Russen which elevates this account from a sordid tale of the abuse of position, to rank it instead as a defining moment in legal history. When Russen came to trial, rape had a far narrower definition than it does in the present day. For instance, rape could be committed only against a woman, and there could be no

rape within marriage, marital status conferring consent. Russen's trial was to have a bearing on a crucial aspect of legislation concerning rape: the necessity of proving penetration.

Twenty-six years after Russen's conviction, the barrister and legal writer Edward Hyde East cites the Russen case in his edition of *The Treatise of the Pleas of the Crown*. This was an occasional publication which listed all crimes with their definitions, and then cited cases which had a bearing on these definitions. East stresses the necessity to prove penetration to secure a conviction for rape, and shows that legal authorities rely on the statement by the judge Edward Coke that 'if there be no penetration, [...] it is no rape', made in his *Institutes of the Lawes of England* (Part Three), published in 1644.[3] It is worth noting that Coke states also that unlawful sex with 'a woman child under the age of ten years with her will, or against her will' constitutes rape – in other words, consent is immaterial in a girl under the age of 10. Russen was arraigned for unlawful sex once with Ann Mayne, and nine times with Sarah Hawkins, when they were 9 years old.

What is so important about Russen's conviction is that Ashhurst gave the jury the task of deciding whether or not there was penetration despite the seeming contradiction of the medical evidence.[4] It would have been easy for him to err on the side of safety and to have ruled there was no penetration, but he did not do so, and the jury decided that there was. As East says, however small the penetration, the commission of rape is 'complete in law'.[5] But Ashhurst was not easy in his mind, and between sentence and execution he gathered the other judges on that Bench and asked them whether he did right in referring the matter to the jury. They discussed it among themselves, and then agreed unanimously that he was right so to do. Sir William Henry Ashhurst thus established in law 'that in such cases the least degree of penetration is sufficient, though it may not be attended with the deprivation of the marks of virginity'.[6]

Victimisation

Another aspect of the trial which is of interest is Russen's defence. Despite having the services of a defence counsel called Chetwood,

Russen seems to take on himself the conduct of his own defence by trying to impress upon the Bench that he is the subject of a conspiracy, for all that his counsel tries to stick to the evidence. When defending himself against the charge of raping Sarah Hawkins, he calls the charge 'a real combination'. Moreover, though his counsel does the right thing by concentrating on the lack of evidence of penetration, the essence of a rape charge, Russen is aggrieved. He believes that he has been let down on the essential point of revealing the conspiracy, which 'would plainly appear, if my counsel had done me justice, and opened the case as it is'. The Bench reminds him that his counsel is not there to state fact, only to question witnesses and to speak on points of law.

Russen's complaint of conspiracy is expressed in his objections to the manner in which the prosecutions are being brought. He tries at one point to claim that the prosecution witnesses are conspiring: 'The witnesses are consulting together that have been examined, telling one another what to say'. As they have already given their evidence, there seems no point to this objection, as is pointed out by the Bench: 'Now their examinations are closed'.

When answering the charge of raping Sarah Hawkins, Russen presents a written statement to the court but is stopped just as he is about to read it. It relates to the first case, that concerning Ann Mayne. Told that he must concentrate on his trial 'for having deflowered one Sarah Hawkins, a child under ten years of age', he blusters: 'I can say no more than that I am falsely accused by Sarah Hawkins'. He goes on to affirm that the version of events given in court is as different from that given before the magistrates 'as light to darkness'.

Curiously Russen cites the contrition of the grandfather of a plaintiff called Harris, who felt compelled to prosecute though the thought of doing so caused him agony. According to Russen, the man admitted to him, '[it] so torments my conscience, that I cannot sleep night or day, but I must do it, or lose my bread'. The problem with this statement, which is pointed out by the Bench, is that there is no plaintiff called Harris. In answer to this, Russen blusters again: 'Justice Wilmot has been ingenious enough to alter the whole scheme'.

Russen claims that David Wilmot is the man behind this conspiracy.

He tells how, when first he was brought before the magistrates, at least three of them 'saw through the evil of it', that he was the subject of a malicious prosecution. Bringing him to court is thus 'nothing now but a piece of spite to try me now for my life'; Wilmot engineered the subsequent three charges of rape made after Ann Mayne's appearance before the magistrates: 'he then made three capital charges more'.

Russen complains that he is 'really used exceeding ill' and that this prosecution has been brought about because of 'a private pique of some of the gentlemen in the parish'. But principally it is Wilmot who is against him. According to Russen, Wilmot tried about a year previously to have him removed from the school 'upon a private pique between him and I', since when Wilmot has pursued Russen 'with all venom in the world'; 'no man living has been used so ill by that gentleman as I have for a whole twelvemonth'.

He claims that Wilmot had been inclined to punish him with the pillory for committing assaults, but then decided that they were capital charges, intending to seek Russen's life. Russen points out that, after his arrest, Wilmot had his assets frozen and his family evicted. Russen had only recently been able to retain the services of his defence counsel.

It seems that Wilmot was turned against him because Russen told off the curate of the parish for keeping bad company, and that the curate told the people in question that Russen 'accused them of being whores and rogues'. He explains that all he did was to point out that 'the man that lives next door to me lives with another man's wife' and that the curate of St Stephen Wallbrook had an illegitimate child. This led to the curate 'and some more of them' persuading 'a deaf, foolish girl' to charge him with rape, and to pretend he had done the same with others. As a result he sought protection in the Tothill Fields Bridewell as a voluntary prisoner.

The judge pronounces on the value of this account: 'I have listened very attentively to all that you have said; I am sorry to say that it does not seem to the point; it seems to point to nothing'. Russen asks that Wilmot be called, which the judge warns him could be dangerous; however, when Russen says that he wants Wilmot asked whether the local curate and that of St Stephen Walbrook made applications to Wilmot against Russen, the judge replies that such a question is 'foreign to this business', and that his local quarrels 'have no connection at all with this subject'.

The claims Russen makes sound paranoid to modern ears, but this kind of factionism was indeed endemic at a local level. This is a time before local government became subject to more organised control, initially by the 1855 Metropolis Management Act, but more completely by the 1899 London Government Act, which created the Metropolitan Boroughs. There was corruption and vested interest in many aspects of parish government, and this can be shown most clearly in the case of one of David Wilmot's enemies, Joseph Merceron, and his activities within the parish of St Matthew, Bethnal Green.

Joseph Merceron

In 1764 Joseph Merceron is born to a silk-weaving family living in Brick Lane; instead of continuing in the weaving trade, Merceron begins work as a clerk in a lottery office, but he is to make his money by building a sizeable portfolio of real estate. David Wilmot is himself a successful local builder who started out as a labourer but, in the year Merceron is born, he enters local politics, resigning most of his building interests to a John Wilmot, who is presumably his son. This is a course Merceron is to follow.

By the time he is 23, Merceron has become the head of a committee to receive church rates, and he is made parish treasurer. In 1795, Merceron becomes a magistrate. He also gathers supporters around him, which will prove invaluable when his corruption finally comes to light. The man who brings Merceron to account is not David Wilmot, however, but the Rector of St Matthew's church, Joshua King.

Until the appointment of King as Rector in 1809, the parish has been served by absentee rectors. It was usual for the rector to install a 'perpetual curate' to do the parish work, while the rector himself would enjoy the stipend from afar. King, however, has serious intentions to get involved in the parish to which he has been appointed, and this means trouble for those such as Merceron, whose practices have so far escaped scrutiny. Indeed, Merceron did resign as parish treasurer when the vestry resolved to audit his accounts, particularly those for the £12,165 voted by parliament in 1800 for relief of the parish. However, he resumed office after securing a vote of thanks for his efforts.

This time he will not be so lucky. King uncovers a web of corruption and fraud among the Parish officials led by Merceron, who is running brothels in many of the local pubs which he has himself licensed, a clear conflict of interests. He is also running protection rackets. It is, however, his manipulation of the Poor Rate that forms the focus of King's efforts.

On 12 June 1813, Merceron is indicted by King, charged with illegal and corrupt alterations in the assessment of the Poor Rate.[7] He is alleged to be lowering the rates due on properties he owns while raising them on others to meet the shortfall. Curiously, the attorney general drops an indictment against Merceron for altering rate books; as a consequence, the trial is abandoned, and an acquittal recorded. King subsequently complains that his solicitor ('the person whom I was so unfortunate as to employ as my solicitor on the occasion') told him not to go to court, and then surrendered the case behind his back.[8]

An audit of Merceron's Poor Rate account carried out the following year, after the resignation of a collector, is rigged with the connivance of his allies. It is thus not revealed that the legal fees from his hearing of June 1813 had been charged to the Poor Rate. In fact, his transport costs were also charged to the Poor Rate; his private account book showed that he debited a total of £925 1s 3d to the fund intended for the relief of the poor of the parish. However, the fraud soon comes to light. A Committee of the House of Commons examines the matter from 1816 to 1817, after which King's party persuades local magistrate Laurence Gwynne to institute legal proceedings against Merceron.

In 1818, Joseph Merceron is removed from his post as parish treasurer, the Bank of England being appointed to act as treasurer instead. He is then prosecuted in the Court of King's Bench for fraud and for re-licensing disorderly public houses, which were his own property. He is convicted, and despite an offer of £10,000 to the prosecution, Merceron is gaoled for eighteen months and fined £200. This is far from the end of the matter though, as the factions in the parish continue their aggression. Merceron's party make counter-allegations of corruption, while eight of Merceron's fellow vestrymen are tried at the King's Bench for conspiracy. At the judge's suggestion, however, this latter case is withdrawn in the interests of reconciliation.

All of this takes its toll on Joshua King's resolve. When King becomes rector of Woodchurch in Cheshire in 1821, the contrast between his new parish, wealthier and less populous than St Matthew's, and the feuding factions in the East End will have become increasingly irresistible. When in 1823, the violence stemming from continuing strife at vestry meetings has escalated such that it has to be suppressed by the reading of the Riot Act, he makes his decision. He wipes the dust of Bethnal Green from his feet and heads for Cheshire, leaving in place his curate, James Mayne.[9] Meanwhile, Merceron resumes his place in local politics, and by 1826 he is chairing vestry committees once more, but will never again be a magistrate.

In his account of Merceron's trials, W.B. Gurney cites the number of affidavits submitted in support of Merceron's character and describes it as unsurprising: such a 'tribute' is 'a service which the practice of the times has rendered a common occurrence'.[10] In his preliminary address to the Court of King's Bench, prosecutor James Scarlett pointed out the number of parish offices Merceron exercised; he reflected that a person so placed 'must also obtain a considerable influence in the parish in which he resided', and that those who would accuse such a person would fear to do so 'for they might apprehend that a gentleman of his influence and authority might crush and oppress' such opposition.[11]

That Benjamin Russen chose to put forward in his defence a variety of revenges to which he felt himself subject goes to show how rife factionism was over forty years prior to the trial of Joseph Merceron the empire builder. It is also indicative of how small-scale local government still was, despite the growth of the burgeoning metropolis. London eventually outgrew this mode of government, though not until the London Government Act was passed in 1899, creating the twenty-eight Metropolitan Boroughs, which became the present-day London Boroughs in 1965.

The future of local government was by no means certain. In 1893 the Royal Commission on the Unification of London recommended unifying London's local government under the recently created London County Council. It was localised resistance to such a centralised approach that caused the second tier of local government to be strengthened by the London Government Act in 1899.

Russen's schoolhouse, where such an important legal precedent was set, no longer exists. It was replaced in 1820 with a new building which, though no longer a schoolhouse, stands yet towards the top of St Matthews Row, having been converted to flats. Joshua King's rectory has been replaced also, with a building dating from 1905. Curiously, the grave of Joseph Merceron is one of only two graves to survive the destruction of the churchyard during an air raid in the Second World War, which also gutted the church. The other grave is that of Peter Renvoize, a fellow Huguenot and crony of Merceron.

Chapter 5

Bethnal House

On the north-eastern side of Bethnal Green Gardens stands a large red brick building which, since 1922, has housed the local library. The more observant viewer, however, will notice that the building isn't in the style of public buildings being erected in the Twenties, and a closer look reveals that the words 'Public Library', and the fancy-work around the door, have been added on; they are not part of the original fabric. In fact, this building dates from 1896 and was erected not as a library, but for another purpose altogether; one which has given rise to the local nickname for Bethnal Green Gardens: Barmy Park.

This was a new dormitory wing for the Bethnal Green Lunatic Asylum, rebuilt substantially in the 1840s but dating back to 1727, when one Matthew Wright took out a lease on Bethnal House, a substantial country house built when literally it was 'all fields round here'. The Asylum closed in 1920, the inmates being transferred to Salisbury in Wiltshire, but not before it had given the name 'Barmy Park' to the green stretching in front of it. A cruel nickname, but it could be argued that they were different times.

After closure, the Asylum buildings were demolished to make way for the Bethnal Green Estate, which still stands to remind the passer-by of how big the Asylum was. The library is the only surviving ward from the hospital; a small cottage also survives, attached to the still extant eastern boundary wall.

Prior to 1727, Bethnal House was a large private residence. Built in the 1570s for John Kirby, a man of affairs in the City of London, it was one of a number of country houses built for merchants and courtiers alike in what would eventually become the East End, but then was largely rural land. Significantly far from the busy riverside

76

settlements with their shipyards and their strange and dangerous populations, inland areas like Bethnal Green were prime locations for the wealthy to build sizeable homes for themselves.

Since the Middle Ages, courtiers and City merchants had established their houses in areas like Stepney and Bethnal Green. Within easy reach of the City, they were surrounded with fields dotted with occasional farms, orchards and market gardens. In 1666, Samuel Pepys brought Admiralty papers and his famed diary to Bethnal House to protect them from the Great Fire of London.

From 1727, Bethnal House grew to become one of the biggest asylums, if not the biggest, in the country. It also gained a reputation for the neglect and maltreatment of its inmates, which would last for a century and would dominate official investigations leading to the regulation of care for the more vulnerable members of society. Like many madhouses, Bethnal House took in two kinds of inmate; its private patients, who brought in proper money, were housed in the Red House, while pauper patients, supported by their parishes, were lodged in the increasingly decaying White House, the original Elizabethan mansion.

As with many madhouses of the period, among the private patients would be 'inconvenient' people shuffled out of the way. Catharine Arnold notes that many such establishments became 'mansions of misery' run by masters 'looking for easy profits and unfettered by legal restrictions'.[1] It is through the experiences of one such that Bethnal House first comes to public notice.

A Citizen Exceedingly Injured
On 9 August 1737 Bryan Payne, a corn chandler on Piccadilly in West London died, leaving behind a widow. By the following March Alexander Cruden, a friend of the Paynes, was paying the widow particular attention. Cruden was a 38-year-old Scottish bookseller and scholar, author of the *Complete Concordance to the Holy Scriptures*. He believed he was making headway with the widow when they had supper together two evenings running and, in his own words, 'his addresses were received chearfully [sic] and pleasantly, without the

least contradiction'.[2] By Friday 17 March though, he was beginning to think that she was toying with him. What he did not suspect was that his dalliance would lead to his being kidnapped in a hackney carriage and bundled off to a private madhouse.

After one abortive attempt to drag Cruden from his home on the grounds that he was mad, he was tricked into a hackney carriage on Thursday 23 March, seemingly on the pretext of taking him to see a fellow Scot at Vauxhall. However, the carriage took him eastwards out of the City and delivered him to Wright's madhouse in Bethnal Green, where Cruden would be imprisoned for more than two months.

Cruden's kidnapping and enforced stay at Bethnal House are recounted in his pamphlet *The London Citizen Exceedingly Injured* which appeared in 1739, a third-person account featuring key elements associated with the madhouse, notably restraint. Cruden's account has not convinced everybody. For Allan Ingram it is 'one of the most engaging pieces of 'mad' writing of the period';[3] 'a coherent and single-minded narrative of events that bears, in spite of the author's intentions, quite a contrary and equally plausible interpretation'.[4] Catharine Arnold sees it as 'a vivid depiction of his allegedly false incarceration',[5] though she does admit that details of his treatment in the account demand 'further investigation'.[6]

Throughout the narrative runs the theme of chains. For the first two nights Cruden is chained to the bedstead, and is only rarely unchained after this. When, after five days confined to his room, he is taken to the public parlour to be with other inmates, he is chained to the chimney-piece. Most of the entries in his day-by-day account end with his being chained to the bedstead at night and having to get in by crawling up from its foot, the chain not being long enough to permit his climbing into it in the usual way.

Chains however are not the only form of restraint he suffers. Two days after arrival, he is confined to a straitjacket, a grim garment which renders the wearer totally vulnerable and, even now, embodies the special restraint applied to the insane. For two days Cruden is subjected to this 'barbarous Usage' day and night, unable to eat except 'with his mouth like a Dog', and scarce able 'to perform the

Necessities of Nature in a becoming manner' (*A London Citizen* p.8). The jacket also prevents him getting any proper sleep. It is only on the Monday that the Under-Keeper John Davis removes the straitjacket during the day, replacing it at night time until, on the Wednesday, Cruden manages to damage it so badly that it is removed for good (there are only two in the whole madhouse).

The relief Cruden feels once the jacket has been removed is palpable. Even though he is now handcuffed regularly, he enjoys 'a happy Deliverance' and 'much inward Peace and Tranquillity' (p.10). He is also able to sleep properly. Henceforth he is allowed out of his room during the day, and even into the garden, but always he has to wear handcuffs and he is still chained up at night. This freedom cannot last however and when, on 26 April, it is discovered that he is smuggling out advertisements to be published in the newspapers complaining about his treatment, he is chained to his bed day and night. His journal entries become variations on that for 28 April: 'The Prisoner being chain'd to the bedstead night and day as before, was only visited by his Keeper *Anna Thomson*, others being denied access' (p.28). Moreover, he cannot now change his trousers: 'his Breeches were never off for the space of five weeks' (p.26).

Apart from three occasions when some friends manage to see him, Cruden receives no visits from his friends from 26 April onwards. This is not because he is ignored, but because his visits are controlled by the same Robert Wightman whom Cruden sees at the heart of the conspiracy to put him, and keep him, in the madhouse. However paranoid Cruden may be seen to be, there is no doubt that Wightman is controlling his confinement. This is reinforced by the letter presented to him for his signature by Wightman on 15 April, absolving him of any wrongdoing: once Cruden has signed this, he will be released. Cruden however saves it, and shows it to various visitors.

Wright, the master of the madhouse, and his wife offer no safeguards, being obedient to those who pay them to accommodate inconvenient people. According to Cruden, Mrs Wright tells him that 'it is their way to execute the Orders of those that pay them', and he observes that the Wrights have 'an insatiable thirst after Money' (p.12).

Wright is portrayed as a bully: at one point tyrannous, at another cajoling. His wife, however, is somewhat more sympathetic. After an initial reserve towards Cruden, she acts after a more kindly fashion.

But Cruden is in the private madhouse, known as the Red House. This is an extension to the White House, the original madhouse established in Kirby's country home. As such, the reader does not get to see those who suffer most at Wright's hands: the paupers. Only once, when invited to visit the Wrights in their quarters, does Cruden get a sight of 'the many miserable Objects of the *White-house*, a Sight exceeding disagreeable to any man of a compassionate disposition' (p.13).

Nevertheless, Cruden experiences the cruelty of the establishment when given medicine on arrival, which he takes against his will lest he be subjected to the 'terrible iron Instrument' (p.7) used to depress the tongue and force down medicine. This detail foreshadows disclosures to come about the force feeding of pauper patients (featured below). Moreover, when Cruden is woken at three in the morning by the 'operation of the said physick' (which is presumably a laxative) and calls for help, not only does Davis not help him, but he comes to Cruden six hours later, at nine o'clock, to handcuff him again, leaving him chained to the bedstead.

It is not just the physical distress of imprisonment that weighs on Cruden; *The London Citizen* is pervaded throughout by a sense of mind-games being played, an active conspiracy controlled by Robert Wightman. Wightman heads a group which Cruden calls the Blind Bench; he is its 'Dictator' (p.18). Certainly Wightman seems to issue and withhold visiting permission. After 26 April, when Cruden is confined to his room, chained to his bed and with the door locked, the only visitors he gets regularly are Anna Thomson the maid, and William Hollowell, the barber's man who shaves him. Otherwise, he is visited by Wightman's 'creatures' who urge him to sign the letter exculpating Wightman's actions.

Fearing being sent to Bedlam, Cruden manages to cut through his bedstead with his dinner knife and escape, though with his chain still attached to his leg and losing a slipper in the process. Despite his physical freedom though, he is not yet free from Wightman's 'Blind

Bench'. When later on the day of his escape he comes before the Lord Mayor at Grocers' Hall, Wightman appears to argue for Cruden's return to confinement. Having shored up his case with letters and other written documents, including testimonies to his reasonable behaviour, Cruden is pursuing his case against Wightman when the journal ends.

Whatever the motivation for his incarceration in Bethnal House, Cruden's account ends with the hope that his experiences will give 'Examples to deter others [from] committing the like Crimes for the time to come' (p.60). Cruden, though, was just one of a number of 'inconvenient people' lodged in Bethnal House, such as Mrs Mills and Mrs Ewbank, whose cases are cited by Catharine Arnold. The *Annual Register* records that on Tuesday 31 March 1772, Mrs Mills was lured to Bethnal House by someone called Gunston on the pretext that her husband was in trouble. On arrival she saw that something was going on, whereupon Gunston 'pushed her into the fore-court, threw her down, and dragged her up the stone steps to the door by her legs'. Once inside she was handcuffed and chained. She was taken to 'a little apartment, the stench of which was intolerable, and the appearance beyond description wretched'.[7]

Mrs Mills was told that her husband had ordered her to be incarcerated; when he visited her two days afterwards he 'declared his sorrow' and took her home. While there however she had met another woman called Mrs Ewbank, whose own husband had ordered her to be put away. After taking out a suit against Gunston, Mrs Mills appealed to Justice John Eardley Wilmot to get Mrs Ewbank released. Wilmot visited Bethnal House and rescued Mrs Ewbank, ordering that those responsible for her treatment be prosecuted. Afterwards he declared that he would not go there again for £5,000: he found the place 'so intolerably nasty, and the stench so abominable'.

Cruden expressed the hope that 'the LEGISLATURE will see the Necessity of bringing in a Bill to regulate *Private Madhouses*'. This was in 1739. It was not until twenty-four years later that a House of Commons Select Committee was set up to look into abuses of the system which allowed sane people to be put away. This led to the passing of an Act in 1774 for Regulating Private Madhouses, requiring all such establishments to be licensed.

A significant problem with the Act was that it excluded paupers from its provision; inmates whose care was paid for by their home parish. As with parish workhouses, the private madhouses provided the absolute minimum for their pauper inmates, and death was often inevitable. Rarely was an inquest held for a dead pauper. The limitations of the 1774 Act, however, prompted the MP George Rose to campaign for a new Act to be passed. He proposed Act after Act, before and after chairing the Select Committee of 1815. By this time of course, Bethnal House had a new Master.

Thomas Warburton
Matthew Wright seems to have died before 1754, because the madhouse was registered in that year to 'Elianor [sic] Wright', presumably his widow. However, it changed hands over the next few years until, on 26 September 1800, after the demise of a Mr Stratton, Bethnal House was acquired as a going concern by Thomas Warburton, owner of Whitmore House, a madhouse in Hoxton, not too far north from Bethnal Green.[8]

An account of the grim conditions at Whitmore House can be found in John Mitford's *A Description of the Crimes and Horrors in the Interior of Warburton's Private Mad-House at Hoxton* (1825), 'a work describing an Establishment of which any honest man would blush to acknowledge himself the patron' (p.iii). If the title does not give sufficient intimation of the tone of the work, it is prefaced with the words of the ghost of Hamlet's father: 'I can a tale unfold, whose lightest word / Will harrow up thy soul' (p.i).

Mitford was an 'inconvenient' person, a relation of a lord who paid £300 for him to be shut up for nine months, and in no mood for caution: 'I will not mince the matter because Mr. Warburton has immense wealth in his hands [...]' (p.2); this is indeed a harrowing tale of the man who takes over the ownership of Bethnal House in 1800. By the time Mitford's exposé was published, however, the Parliamentary Select Committee had brought to official view the extent of the abuse and neglect rife within England's madhouses, shining a strong light on Thomas Warburton's dark doings.

In 1815, the Select Committee's *Report* was published, giving the minutes of evidence heard at the conclusion of its investigation.[9] These minutes contain interesting details not only about what was going on at Warburton's Hoxton and Bethnal Green establishments, but also some insight into how slackly such places were monitored by the Commissioners appointed under the 1774 Act.

The Select Committee of 1815
On 8 June 1815, Dr Richard Powell, Secretary to the Commissioners, gives evidence before the Select Committee and has to account for the lack of follow-up concerning faults recorded in the minute book of the Commissioners. Surrendered on 11 May, it recorded every fault found with the madhouses inspected: 'and there are many noticed in that book' (p.234).

Asked about the overcrowding problem at the White and Red Houses at Bethnal Green, Powell takes it on trust that this will have been addressed: 'We have not since visited the house, but we have always found Mr Warburton ready to remedy any inconveniences complained of'. Powell's trust in Warburton is founded on 'experience in former cases', and remains unshaken despite Rose taking him through inspection minutes as far back as December 1812 to show how the overcrowding issue has never been properly addressed by Warburton.

Powell's responses are uncertain: 'I suppose it was done of course' (p.282); 'I think that is the case'; 'I cannot answer that question from my recollection' (p.283). This failure to follow-up is shown most tellingly in the case of a 19-year-old female inmate of Bethnal Green deemed potentially sane by the Commissioners. They directed him to contact her friends to recommend that she be reassessed, but Powell has no idea what happened afterwards: 'I do not recollect; it was in 1811' (p.284), i.e. only three and a half years previously.

When Warburton himself is called to answer on 30 June, he assures Lord Robert Seymour (in the chair) that he attended to everything.

Answering the charge that, in December 1810, overcrowding left some female fever patients lying on the floor, he answered that 'it is impossible for any person to go round any establishment where there are 100 lunatics, and not see a number of them voluntarily throwing themselves down in different positions, and in different directions' (p.354).

His casual, even glib answer is typical of Warburton's defensive attitude, i.e. to deny everything and to throw the burden back on the questioner. He denies outright the records of overcrowding noticed on visits carried out in May 1814 and January 1815: there 'must have been a gross mistake' (p.350). He is taxed with the accommodation for paupers in the Red House: it is 'infamously bad' and requires 'immediate reform'; Warburton replies 'I should conceive it impossible', 'there must have been some error' (p.351). In his own eyes Warburton is a caring master making every provision for the paupers in his care: what else could any criticisms of his regime be but errors?

The problems identified at Bethnal Green are problems which the Committee finds endemic to England's private madhouses. The Committee's report identifies a number of problems with the system as it stands: chronic overcrowding, lack of staff, lack of medical attention to their mental health, excessive use of restraint, mistreatment and neglect, and the 'detention of persons, the state of whose minds did not require confinement' (pp.3-4).

John Rogers

When the Select Committee reconvenes in 1816 to examine additional evidence in support of its conclusion that the 1774 Act is insufficient, and that a revised Act is required, Bethnal House dominates the hearing. A damning witness is the apothecary John Rogers, a regular attendant at Bethnal House while assistant to its medical attendant John Dunston, son-in-law to Thomas Warburton.

In 1815 Rogers published *A Statement of the Cruelties, Abuses, and Frauds, Which Are Practised in Mad-Houses*. Dedicated to George Rose, it describes, without naming names, the cruelties inflicted 'by

1. Bethnal Green watch house, Wood Close, where Ann Ashley suffered in November 1828. (Alan Tucker)

2. The former *King and Queen* public house, Cheshire Street, where the inquest was held into Ann Ashley's death. (Alan Tucker)

3. The *Salmon and Ball* public house, Cambridge Heath Road, outside which John Valline and John Doyle were hanged in December 1769. (Alan Tucker)

4. The former *Dolphin* public house, Redchurch Street, where a cutters' meeting was disturbed in September 1769, resulting in three deaths. (Alan Tucker)

5. Crispin Street, looking north to where Lewis Chauvet's handkerchief manufactory once stood (beneath the 1920s extension of Spitalfields Market). (Alan Tucker)

6. Hare Street sign – it was in a brick field off Hare Street (now Cheshire Street) that Daniel Clarke was lynched in April 1771. (Alan Tucker)

7. Behind Tesco, Bethnal Green Road, is the site of Wilmot Square: it was facing Wilmot Square that John Gamble was hanged in July 1780. (Alan Tucker)

8. Black Lion House, Whitechapel Road, covers Black Lion Yard where the *Red Lion* public house was attacked in June 1780. (Alan Tucker)

9. West Dock, St Katharine's Docks, covers St Catherine's Lane where John Lebarty's public house was attacked in June 1780. (Alan Tucker)

10. Virginia Street, where Joseph Brown was beaten nearly to death by Randolph Branch and William Descent in August 1752. (Alan Tucker)

11. Wellclose Square, from the site of Princes Square; here Edward Holt was attacked by Randolph Branch and William Descent in August 1752, but their attack was thwarted by neighbours. (Alan Tucker)

12. The memorial to the Ulrika Eleanora Church in Swedenborg Gardens is the only reminder of Princes Square, where Peter Conway and his accomplices bought two pistols, but no bullets, from Robert Dunn in May 1770. (Alan Tucker)

13. The Church of St Dunstan and All Saints, Stepney, near which John Chambers, master of Ratcliff Workhouse, was attacked and robbed by William Paterson and three accomplices in December 1769. (Alan Tucker)

14. The former St Matthews Church School, St Matthew's Row, replaced the 1763 school over which Benjamin Russen presided until convicted of rape in October 1777. (Alan Tucker)

15. The grave of Joseph Merceron, St Matthew's Churchyard. Convicted of fraud in 1818, he returned from prison to resume his place in local politics. (Alan Tucker)

16. The Rectory, St Matthew's, Bethnal Green; the original rectory housed Joshua King, nemesis of Joseph Merceron until King retired from London in 1823. (Alan Tucker)

17. A former dormitory wing, all that remains of Bethnal House Asylum; now Bethnal Green Library. (Alan Tucker)

18. Boundary stone marking the grounds of Bethnal House Asylum rebuilt by John Warburton. (Alan Tucker)

19. The former Reflection Works, Cheshire Street, site of Bethnal Green parish workhouse from which Judith Defour took her daughter Mary in January 1734. (Alan Tucker)

20. The site of Boar's Head Yard, next to Goulston Street, where Joseph Lipman died of neglect in July 1870. (Alan Tucker)

21. Sandys Row, looking toward the approximate site of Number 29, where the body of Matilda Hewson's newborn child was found in September 1847. (Alan Tucker)

22. Site of former Old Gravel Lane Bridge, and former dock wall at Tobacco Dock, where in December 1883 James Williams tried to commit suicide. (Alan Tucker)

23. The former Bethnal Green Police Station, Bethnal Green Road, on the steps of which John Parr shot dead his fiancée Sarah Willett in August 1900. (Alan Tucker)

24. The former London Hospital Medical College, Turner Street; the likely location of the inquest into the death of Emma Smith in April 1888. (Alan Tucker)

25. The entrance to George Yard (now Gunthorpe Street) through which Martha Tabram passed on her way to her violent death in August 1888. (Alan Tucker)

26. All that remains of Thrawl Street, on which the house stood where Frederick Jewitt regained consciousness after being chloroformed in January 1850. (Alan Tucker)

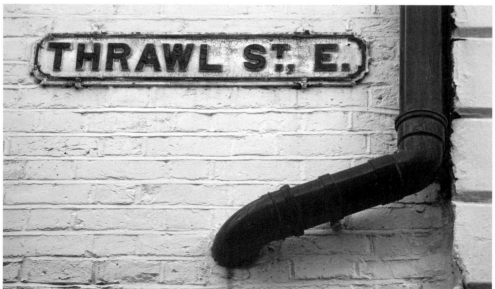

27. The site of Shadwell Police Station, on the corner of Juniper Street and King David Lane, where Susannah Field was taken after attempting to poison her mother in January 1891. (Alan Tucker)

28. The site of the Pavilion Theatre, Whitechapel Road, where James Elphinstone was performing when Martha Sharp sent him a jam tart laced with Spanish fly in July 1850. (Alan Tucker)

certain licensed ruffians' on their unfortunate charges in order to rouse his readers 'to a sense of obvious duty' (pp.7-8). Now, before the Select Committee, he is far more explicit. His evidence is the first to be given in the *Minutes of Evidence* published in 1816.[10]

Rogers, described by John Mitford as having been 'dismissed for his humanity' from Whitmore House (*Crimes and Horrors* p.2), has much to testify about the treatment of the inmates of Bethnal House, supported by the evidence of his sister Mrs Mary Humieres, former housekeeper at the White House, managed by Matthew Talbot. Such is the impact of these testimonies that Talbot arranges for ten affidavits to be sworn by himself, his wife and others in refutation of the allegations made, and for them to be published, so that his 'character' might be submitted 'to the decision of an impartial public'.[11] He appends a report which details how Rogers tried to evade a debt of £500 borrowed from Talbot to undermine his character further.

One of the villains of Bethnal Green is a keeper whom Rogers and Humieres call Samuel Ramsbotham, though his real name appears to be Rambard. Rogers and his sister cite the case of Captain Dickinson, a former captain in the Royal Navy who, while handcuffed and chained by the legs, was beaten by Rambard. Another victim of beating by the same keeper was a farmer called Driver; Humieres describes seeing Rambard 'beating him with a pair of boots in a most dreadful manner' (p.81).

While Rogers states that 'I frequently witnessed his striking patients, hundreds of times' (p.2), Talbot denies having ever received any complaints about Rambard's mistreating patients, though he confesses that Rambard did hit a patient in a straitjacket once who had bit his hand. He even denies all knowledge of Driver being an inmate: 'I have had five thousand patients in that house since I came there, and I cannot remember their names'. Warburton denies ever having heard of any complaints about Rambard's behaviour, endorsing him as 'a man that I had a very good opinion of' (p.38).

Another cruel keeper seems to have been a Betty Welch. She is accused of forcing a Mrs Elliot to eat salt when feeding her to make her thirsty and encourage her to drink; Rogers also testifies to having seen signs that Elliot had been beaten. Typically, Talbot claims that Mrs Elliot was injured in a fall while being confined in a straitjacket: 'accidents of that sort will occur in confining a patient' (p.17). Humieres also testifies that on the orders of Talbot, Betty Welch confined an Isabella Adams in her crib bed and horsewhipped her; Humieres saw 'the blood follow the strokes' (p.82).

One dangerous practice rife in madhouses at the time was the practice of 'forcing', i.e. force-feeding patients who refused to eat. Rogers testifies (p.4) to the manner of 'forcing' used at Bethnal House, the jaws being opened with 'a large key' and the food fed through a vessel looking like a teapot. The nose and mouth are obstructed, such that 'in this state the patient must either swallow or die'. He is graphic in his descriptions of those who have resisted swallowing 'till they have been upon the point of death', and believes that in Bethnal House the vessel's spout is too long, and is poked in too far, so that 'the food passes down the wind-pipe, and suffocation ensues'.

One Mrs Hodges seems to have suffocated while being force-fed 'water-gruel' by another keeper, Mary Seale. Mary Humieres also tells of a man being taken upstairs by Sam Rambard and subjected to a forcing. She testifies that the inmate 'called several times for Mr Talbot to come up for God's sake, or he should be killed'; Talbot refused, despite his wife's entreaties, and soon Sam came downstairs: the patient had died 'in a fit' (p.86).

A gruesome story is told connected with another problem at Bethnal House: exposure to the cold. Rogers testifies to having taken off the toes of pauper patients, and once having taken off the feet of a 19-year-old pauper girl because of mortification (i.e. gangrene). Had Rogers been alerted earlier this might have been prevented, but though he tried to save her feet, he 'took the whole of the toes off near the instep, so that she could not walk' (p.13). The almost routine nature of the incident makes it all the more gruesome: 'it was a common occurrence in the house'; 'when I went in, I performed it without saying a word to any body'.

Over and again, Rogers and his sister are asked whether they complained about the cases they have brought in to evidence, and they reply that they remonstrated about the levels of neglect and misuse at Bethnal House, but felt it pointless to complain about individual cases. Moreover, no inquests are held into the deaths of paupers. Rogers claims that the coroner is only called 'when they cut their throat, or hang themselves, or die in any way by their own hands', and even then it is not guaranteed an inquest will be held (p.5).

Despite the evidence put together by the Select Committee hearings of 1815 and 1816, no progress is made in terms of passing an Act to improve the situation for pauper patients in England's madhouses. And then something happens to focus attention again on Bethnal House and its proprietor Thomas Warburton.

The Infirmary

In August 1826 John Hall and the Reverend Birdwood, two directors of the poor of the Parish of Marylebone, call at the White House to carry out an inspection. The parish has a long relationship with this house, having renewed its verbal contract with the establishment when Warburton took it over in 1800. Birdwood and Hall are there to see the paupers belonging to their parish who are in the care of Thomas Jennings, who succeeded Talbot as manager of the White House around 1818.

Jennings is not there so his wife takes the two directors to the female side, where all the female paupers of their parish are presented to them. A keeper then takes them to the male side, where they are shown all but one of the males. He is in the infirmary, but will be with them directly. That there is an infirmary in the male side is news to the directors, and the Marylebone apothecary William Goodger will come under criticism later for not knowing about it.

After some moments, Hall and Birdwood become impatient with the delay and decide to go straight to the infirmary. This causes the keeper to hesitate: it is usual practice to bring the pauper inmates to those who want to see them. There is more behind this hesitancy, though, than a breach of custom. As Birdwood and Hall climb the stairs, they see the missing pauper making slow progress towards them, being supported as he comes. They are soon to see why he was not to be inspected in the infirmary.

When they enter the infirmary, they find a room Hall describes later as 'exceedingly oppressive, from the excrement and the smell which existed there' (p.15).[12] Later he will state that this is not the smell from the evacuation of an incontinent patient, but that of neglect: 'I have been in the habit of visiting hospitals and workhouses a good deal, but I never witnessed anything to equal that' (p.122). So rank is the air that he has to hold his breath while he casts his eye quickly over the grim sight.

Hall is unable to stay there long; as for Birdwood, he is off down the stairs before Hall is forced to give up his scrutiny. But for all the noxious state of the room, Hall is able to take in most of the detail before retreating, and what he sees shocks him. It contains 'wet patients': incontinent patients, an explanation of the smell and the excrement. They are not in bed though, but are sitting on benches, several patients being chained to the wall.

Unsurprisingly, the discovery that the White House has an infirmary in the male side, and that it is in such a condition, leads to 'some conversation' among the Board of Guardians and Directors of the Poor for the parish, which becomes all the more urgent after the discharge from the White House of a parishioner called William Solomon, who reveals much about the treatment of the inmates, particularly the wet patients. Another visit is planned, to see whether anything else untoward has been concealed from official visitors. On 26 February 1827, Hall travels back to Bethnal Green accompanied by another director called Pepys and by Lord Robert Seymour. In order that nothing might be concealed, they arrive unannounced on, or just after, half past seven.

Jennings is there, and is in no mood to be ordered around. He stands his ground: it's very late in the evening to be calling. Lord Robert presses him, pointing out that not only are they Guardians of the Poor, but he is also a magistrate, and that moreover it is only a quarter to eight, but Jennings will not give in. After all, the patients will be in bed, and they wouldn't wish to go inspecting female patients in their beds 'at this time of night', surely? It is clear that the house is not shut down for the night since there is activity going on, including the delivery of a coffin; but realising that they are getting nowhere the party retires.

Subsequently Thomas Warburton is summoned before the Board at the Marylebone Workhouse where he states that he would rather give up the Marylebone paupers than be subjected to such all-hours visits. The Board then removes its paupers from the White House and transfers them to a house in Hoxton run by a Sir Jonathan Miles, who is quite prepared to allow visits at any time. Warburton may have won a small victory here, albeit at the loss of nine shillings a week per pauper, but this withdrawal is to have repercussions. Marylebone is not the only parish to keep paupers at the White House.

The Crib Rooms

As the Marylebone paupers are being withdrawn, the news reaches the Parish of St George, Hanover Square, which, like Marylebone, has had a verbal contract with Bethnal House extending beyond 1800. A party is despatched to the White House with instructions to inspect every part. Richard Roberts, assistant to the overseers and parish officers, requests Jennings to show the party the entire establishment, particularly the parts with which the party from Marylebone found such fault. Jennings is friendly this time, and is delighted to show the infirmary, which has been cleaned out thoroughly since the previous visit.

It is not until Roberts and his party return to make their report to the board, which is then compared with the experiences of former inmates, that they realise they have been deceived. An unannounced visit is then made, taking the former inmates along to ferret out the missed places. Again Jennings is not there, but his wife is, and she permits them, in the attendance of a keeper, to be taken wherever the former inmates will. They find the crib rooms.

The crib is a wooden bedframe containing straw and covered with a blanket; it is intended for accommodating wet patients. The entrance to the male crib rooms is hard to see if you do not know it is there; in a dark, shady corner, it is 'certainly not intended to be very visible' (p.30). What perplexes Roberts, however, is that these rooms were known to the parish some ten or twelve years before, but over time they have been forgotten.

The rooms Roberts and his companions find are not as filthy as the infirmary when it was discovered by Birdwood and Hall, but they are crowded with cribs and not well ventilated. This time Jennings does not object when Roberts makes a return visit to see the patients in bed – he can even inspect the female ones; subsequently Warburton makes an arrangement with St George's that they may visit any time they want. The removal of the Marylebone patients maybe had a bigger impact than Warburton expected.

Given that they are used for wet patients, the drawbacks of the crowded and ill-ventilated crib room can be imagined. Former patient William Solomon reveals that the cribs are also used for 'high patients', those who suffer fits and rages. Before being locked down for the night, he claims, the patients are required to strip naked; they are then locked down, not by regular keepers but by recovering patients. This leaves them vulnerable to abuse by these convalescents, who are liable to become irritated by their charges. What is more, there is no supervision at night, and no opportunity to summon assistance should anything happen.

The patients confined to the cribs are chained down before dusk and not released until the morning; at weekends they are chained down around three o'clock on Saturday afternoon and not released until Monday morning. They are thus kept in bed 'without being unchained or allowed to get up to relieve themselves in any way whatever' (p.32). The consequent need for deep cleaning on Monday is answered by taking the naked inmates, putting them in a tub (presumably one at a time: there is no evidence whether the water is changed after each one) and then swabbed down with a mop. At least the men are; a former inmate called Ann Gibbons testifies that female patients are 'washed in a pail' (p.39).

The revelations at Bethnal Green, and the attempts to conceal them, stir up sufficient concern for another Select Committee to sit in 1827 in order to foreground the call for the establishment of a county lunatic asylum, a public establishment free from the personal interest which bedevils the private madhouses. The primary example of the dangers of the private madhouse advanced by the Committee will be the Bethnal Green Madhouse, the White House in particular.

The Select Committee of 1827
The Committee hears evidence from representatives of the parishes of Marylebone, St Pancras, and St George, Hanover Square. It hears also from former patients at the White House who confirm that overcrowding, confinement and lack of supervision are rife. As well as grim details of the crib rooms, statements are made about the lack of proper diet and the interception of letters.

The hearing opens on Thursday 14 June; it is not until Monday 18 June that the focus is directed to Bethnal Green, evidence from parish officers establishing the verbal contracts between Warburton and the parishes whose paupers he receives. On the following day, Tuesday 19 June, Thomas Warburton is called before the Committee. As in 1816, he begins with bluster.

Before he enters, a lengthy statement is read out, submitted in advance by Warburton to answer the charges made against him in the evidence heard over the Thursday and Friday. This statement begins by accusing the Committee of treating him unfairly, then lists twenty-two witnesses, as well as others whose names he does not have yet, whom he would like to have examined before he goes on to answer the charges he has found in the statements of evidence.

When he comes before the Committee, however, Warburton is far less confident. He begins with the claim that, 'I am not aware of any complaint made by the commissioners, unless it be that of the house being too full', but when confronted with records of complaints in the minutes of the commissioners, his denials sound petulant: 'It may appear in their books, but it was never made personally to me, or to my assistant, to my recollection [...] Such complaint has never been made to me personally, and I am not permitted to see their minutes' (p.67). He shores up this mulishness with the repeated statement that he is not able to remember complaints being made. Also he seems unable to remember details about the running of his establishment, and retorts often that the Committee must ask other people for their answers.

Robert Gordon, in the Chair, is determined to break through this stubborn denial and, by piling fact upon fact, he manages to elicit some damaging admissions from Warburton, such as his unrealistic assertion that his son-in-law Dr Dunston is able to discharge his duties properly. As sole medical attendant for Warburton's 800 patients housed at Bethnal Green and at Whitmore House in Hoxton, Dunston is also the surgeon at St Luke's hospital.

Gordon manages to unsettle Warburton's seeming sense of security. There is a telling moment when he presses the question whether Warburton considers it necessary that violent patients in the crib rooms should be confined from Saturday evening until Monday morning. Warburton tries to evade the question, and runs out of bluster:

> – They were not confined under my direction certainly.
> Do you consider it necessary? – [*The Witness hesitated.*]
> Do you decline to answer the question? – I do.
>
> (p.79)

This leads swiftly to an admission that he never visited the crib rooms: 'Certainly I never did; I left them to the management of Mr Jennings'.

Warburton has been distancing himself from blame, admitting that his assurances that all is well at the White House are based not on his own knowledge, but on his trust in the manager: 'I have such confidence in the superintendent, Mr Jennings' (p.74). Self-preservation seems to be leading Warburton to abandon Jennings and retreat behind a wall of denial. He does not deny that such confinement is happening in the crib rooms, he admits that Jennings has been keeping the practice from him.

From here, Gordon is able to undermine the Master's expressions of confidence in his manager. He asks, 'is it not extremely possible that Mr Jennings may have concealed other abuses from you?'

Warburton has to reply, 'I think it possible' (p.80). Gordon then asks whether Warburton intends to retain Jennings as manager of the White House, a daring question since there has been no hint of any such doubt, but clearly Gordon understands Warburton, who replies, 'Perhaps I may, but I have not made up my mind as to that'. This admission will be a tool which Gordon can use when on the next day he is able to question Jennings himself.

His unsettling experience before Gordon clearly has an effect on Warburton. The following day, after Jennings has given his evidence, John Warburton is called to give evidence because of his father's 'indisposition'. The son's answers are more considered, and the phrase 'I believe' begins to qualify his statements as Gordon's questions become more probing, and towards the end of his evidence, he is giving yes/no answers. Significantly he admits with a single 'yes' that he depends entirely on Jennings for his knowledge of the treatment of the patients in the crib room, as he has never visited it on a Sunday, or seen the confined cases released on a Monday. When, on the following day, medical attendant John Dunston gives his evidence, Gordon is quick to establish that Dunston too relies largely on Jennings: 'If I do not happen to see a case, it is pointed out to me' (p.103).

When Jennings, the man on whom everyone seems to rely, gives his evidence, his poor management of the White House becomes obvious. The Committee are looking to discredit the private establishments, and Jennings' mismanagement of the White House provides the best means to illustrate the evils of the present system. Apart from the treatment of the crib room patients, there are more overarching problems with the White House.

One of them is the unhealthy lack of 'classification', the separation of different kinds of patient which Jennings claims is at the heart of his curative approach. The male pauper patients are divided into three rooms but, under questioning, Jennings admits that they are not kept confined into their appropriate rooms; instead they are able to wander around and mingle with each other: 'Then there is no classification in your day rooms?' 'Not shut up completely' (p.85).

The danger of mingling is expressed in the account of the teenage boy from Barking, given on 28 June by Sir James Williams, a director of the poor in St Pancras parish. The boy had a temporary fever after a soaking, but was bundled off to the White House and 'put with people that were as mad as could be'; indeed, the sight of some five or six men struggling to restrain a patient Sir James thought 'enough to make the boy mad' (p.186).

This mingling is a consequence of overcrowding, and of an inadequate level of supervision and inspection. The Committee establish that the number of keepers has been as low as two in the past and that, despite the denials of Warburton and Jennings, convalescent patients have been employed as assistant keepers. The questioning of Jennings also elicits the lack of record keeping, and the consequent inability to maintain the establishment and its patients properly.

This has an inevitable effect on the inmates' diet, important to the physical and mental health of the patients. If no records are kept as to diet, how can John Dunston be sure that the correct diets are administered to patients with special requirements?

The report to which these statements of evidence are appended states that its investigation has shown that 'Mr. Warburton's Establishment has hitherto been considered as good as the generality of licensed Houses' which receive London's pauper patients (p.3). However, this is not to the credit of the White House; rather it has shown that the 'abuses in the management of the Houses for the reception of Lunatics' highlighted by the Select Committee of 1815 are still prevalent. This is followed by twenty-two recommendations.

John Warburton

The Select Committee's findings led in large measure to the passing of the Madhouses Act of 1828, revised in 1832, which started the practice of opening up private madhouses to regular public scrutiny. However, the findings seem to have had a detrimental effect on Thomas Warburton: the faltering witness, who declined to answer Gordon's question and retired to be represented by his son, was a feeble version of the brash, self-confident witness of 1816. At some point between the Select Committee's report and the passing of the Act, his son John took over control of both the White and Red Houses. Then in 1836 Thomas Warburton died, leaving his madhouses along with everything else to his son.

John Warburton's regime at Bethnal Green was an enlightened one. Indeed, Appendix G of the 1847 *Further Report of the Commissioners in Lunacy* catalogues improvements carried out by Warburton since 1829, such as giving tasks to the patients and the provision of a library.[13] In 1832 the White House became exclusively female, with male patients moved to the Red House, and in 1842 building work began; soon the whole place would be rebuilt as a single institution.

The improvements were brought about with the particular assistance of an out-of-work naval surgeon and Arctic explorer called Charles Beverly. With his help, Warburton was able to transform his establishment. Elaine Murphy claims in her biographical study of Warburton and Beverly that 'this huge and important institution was transformed over 15 years into one of the best by two determined men'.[14]

So proactive did the new madhouse become that in 1844 the *Report of the Metropolitan Commissioners in Lunacy* states that a well-behaved pauper, when discharged as cured, may return to Bethnal House for meals and a bed while looking for work, for fear the pauper should 'be soon sent back under a relapse brought on by destitution' if cast onto the streets.[15] At last the dark days of Bethnal House were no more.

Chapter 6

Undone by Poverty

The thought of East End poverty brings to mind grim scenes of nineteenth century slums, but of course poverty has been ever present. Inevitably the continuous development during the eighteenth century of the riverside areas and those on the fringe of the City brought financial difficulties. It was the eighteenth century that saw the development of relief for bankrupts, beginning with the 1705 Bankrupts Act. This act allowed bankrupts relief and discharge of their debts, provided the debtors surrender all their assets and submit to regular inspection. However this came with a severe punishment for those who tried to defraud it: death without benefit of clergy.

John Restow

This was the price paid by the first person to be discovered trying to defraud the Act.[1] John Restow was a linen draper of Whitechapel who, by 10 December 1710, had become so heavily in debt that he had himself declared bankrupt. He was reluctant, however, to lose hold of what the trial record calls his 'Shop Goods and Household Goods', to the value of £500. So on the night of 10 December, he put all his effects into carts and took them to the riverside where there was a hoy (a small coasting boat) riding at anchor. Restow went aboard with his goods; the hoy weighed anchor and made its way downriver in the darkness.

Unlike today's Thames, the eighteenth-century river was heavily used, and Restow must have been wondering whether any of the vessels they passed would come alongside and disgorge officials to seize both him and his possessions. He need not have worried; not yet, anyway. Eventually they arrived at Leigh-on-Sea, at that time a thriving maritime town. Within a few hours fishing boats would be coming in, bringing their catches for the fishwives to gut; among the many other craft on the river was a sloop. It was in this that Restow and his possessions were to be taken abroad.

How far Restow managed to get from Leigh before he was taken is not recorded, but his creditors arrested him aboard ship and brought him back to London. They'd been tipped off, and had traced his movements. His case came before the Old Bailey sessions more than five anxious months later, on 16 May 1711. Restow does not deny the charge: maybe he hoped for mercy, or some kind of clemency. If he did, he was cruelly disappointed; he was condemned and sentenced to hang.

Other legislation was to follow, and in 1748 an Act for the Relief of Insolvent Debtors was passed, after some amendment, by Parliament. This was intended not only to get people out of debtors' prison, but also to encourage merchants and craftsmen, as well as mariners and merchant seamen, back to the country they had fled to avoid being seized by their creditors. Benefit of the Act could be claimed by fugitives from debt who were abroad before 1 January 1748. Once again though, the penalty for fraud was death, a penalty risked that summer by Shadwell innkeeper William Montgomery.[2]

William Montgomery
In 1747, William Montgomery has the *Highlander Inn*, at the bottom of Fox Lane, Lower Shadwell (covered nowadays by the King Edward Memorial Park). According to his own words[3] he went to sea when he was about 13 years old, both his father and mother being dead, and sailed to the East and West Indies, to most parts of France, to Spain and around the Mediterranean. All the while he saved money, and, on his return, he settled in Bishopsgate Street and married. Soon the couple moved to Shadwell when he acquired the *Highlander*, which he left to his wife to manage during his occasional trips to the Netherlands. There is no explanation given for these trips, but it is possible that he was smuggling; perhaps bringing in spirits for the inn.

In December 1747 they have a servant called Isabella Hannah who, on 22 December, goes to William Smith's house, which is within twenty yards of the *Highlander*, to order drink for the inn. While there she asks for her Christmas box, a common custom; Smith gives her half a crown. Shortly, she comes back, saying that Montgomery will not take half a crown, so Smith gives her another sixpence. Later, Isabella remembers a Peter Peterson, lodging at the *Highlander* in 1744, and dining with William Montgomery at his house on Christmas Day. These might seem like insignificant details; certainly Montgomery seems to have forgotten them by the following summer. Forgetting them, and what he is doing on New Year's Eve, will cost him his life.

On 27 December, a John Ward is drinking flip with a friend at the *Highlander* (flip in those days being a mixture of beer, rum and sugar heated with a red hot poker to make it froth, or flip). Too much is consumed perhaps, because things turn nasty and the pair square up for a fight. Ward is clearly drunk though, and the others in the bar will not allow the fight. The two men agree to meet at the same place on New Year's Eve to settle the matter. By then their heads will have cleared, and they may make it up in the meantime.

When Ward arrives at the *Highlander* on 31 December he sees Montgomery, seemingly made jovial by drink and the mood of the day. Montgomery expresses his surprise to Ward, not knowing him to be a fighting man. Whether he is or not, Ward will drink the Old Year out and the New Year in apparently without incident. However, on settling down at the back of the inn he sees a man called Thomas Weymore sitting with his back to the partition and drinking punch, though Weymore doesn't see him.

Weymore is a creditor of Montgomery's, as is the aforementioned William Smith, and they are both being entertained at the *Highlander* by Montgomery, in a little back room of the inn. They are regaled with three bowls of punch, which Montgomery makes himself, and which he drinks with them. Just as Smith supplies the Highlander with alcohol, so Weymore supplies bread, but he has instructed his people not to deliver any more until the innkeeper clears what he owes. In fact, Weymore asks for his money that evening, but it will not be until later in the New Year that he gets paid, and only then because he blackmails Montgomery into paying up.

The two creditors will stay until sometime between eleven and twelve o'clock that night. At about seven o'clock, however, one Daniel Goodwin arrives. Weymore has already lent him money to carry on a lawsuit, but it is Goodwin's birthday, so he comes to borrow a little more to celebrate. On entering the inn and heading for the back room, Goodwin sees Montgomery going up the steps before him, carrying a bowl of punch.

A fortnight after New Year's Day, Isabella Hannah leaves the service of the Montgomerys; William Montgomery is at home when she leaves.

On 22 July 1748 a warrant is signed by the Lord Mayor of London, Sir Robert Ladbroke, to let all the creditors of William Montgomery know that he has surrendered himself into the hands of the warden of the Fleet Prison as a fugitive from debt. He intends to take an oath at Guildhall that he was abroad on 1 January 1748; he intends also to take the benefit of the Act for the Relief of Insolvent Debtors and escape a lengthy stretch in debtors' prison.

The Act was passed earlier that year. Providing for the release from prison of debtors whose debts extended back before January 1748, it allowed a similar benefit to debtors who had fled abroad to avoid their creditors; this was in order to attract such fugitives back to their country's service. To claim the benefit of the Act, they had to have been abroad on or before 1 January 1748, and they must return and surrender themselves to a debtors' prison.[4]

Montgomery is in a bad way. Since the New Year celebrations his wife has died. Soon after this his inn folded; seemingly his suppliers refused to stretch his credit any further. Leaving the pub business, he has remarried; having taken a house in Nightingale Lane (now Thomas More Street), off East Smithfield, he and his wife let out lodgings to sailors, and to anyone else with the price of a room.

By making his declaration that he was out of the country he intends to clear his pressing debts, but by so doing Montgomery has embarked on a perilous, even foolhardy path. The warrant signed on 22 July states clearly that he was 'beyond the seas' on 1 January 1748. Clearly he has forgotten New Year's Eve at the *Highlander*, as well as Christmas dinner with Peter Peterson.

The September sessions at the Guildhall begin on the fifth; Montgomery appears on the twenty-seventh and takes his oath that he was in Rotterdam on 1 January 1748; having delivered up a list of all his creditors and a schedule of debts, he receives the benefit of the Act as a fugitive. Thomas Weymore does not attend; he is no longer a creditor. Lest he give evidence about the New Year's Eve drink, he was paid by Mrs Montgomery while her husband was on one of his trips to the Netherlands. In fact Daniel Goodwin said to him before the hearing that he intended to mention it, but was hushed up by Weymore: 'Hold your tongue, I am satisfied'. For reasons he does not specify, William Smith does not attend as a creditor despite being owed '£47 and upwards'.

William Montgomery is granted the benefit of the Act. This appears to have been a short-lived respite however. In the four years before his deception at the Guildhall comes to light, he is to experience more difficulties. Having got together money from his lodging house in Nightingale Lane, he opens a slop shop, selling ready-made clothing. This is managed mainly by his wife, while Montgomery continues to supplement his income by taking his trips to the Netherlands.

Despite this activity, he finds himself confined for debt in both the Whitechapel and Marshalsea Prisons, and is in prison in September 1752 for a debt owed to a Mr Smith, possibly the William Smith who was a creditor in 1747. And then, on 26 October, William Montgomery is indicted at the Old Bailey Sessions for deception, intending to cheat and defraud his creditors four years previously.

In court, Montgomery insists that he was in Rotterdam before 1 January 1748 and was still there later in the month. He gets his friend Peter Peterson to swear that he saw Montgomery in Rotterdam in late December and early January. Evidence is given by his former maid

Isabella Hannah, however, that not only was Montgomery at home on 22 December, and made her go back to William Smith for an extra sixpence for her Christmas box, but also that Peterson actually dined with Montgomery at the *Highlander* on Christmas Day. That he was not out of the country is confirmed by a neighbour from Fox Lane, Elizabeth Murrey.

Montgomery brings a number of witnesses in his defence, principally character witnesses, although Jane Underwood, a creditor of his, testifies that she believes he was in Rotterdam 'as much as I do that I am here now'. One Eleanor Scot testifies that she journeyed to the Netherlands with him in 1749 and found him very familiar with the place; however, given his frequent trips there, this does not really signify. In the face of evidence given by William Smith, Thomas Weymore, John Ward and Daniel Goodwin, it is no surprise that Montgomery is found guilty. He is sentenced to death, and some days later the date of his execution is given as Monday 13 November.

The Ordinary of Newgate, the prison chaplain, spends much time with Montgomery while he awaits execution.[5] Though he maintains his innocence for some time, his approaching death seems to break down his confidence. On the afternoon of Friday 10 November he tells the Ordinary that he meant to sail to Rotterdam, but was prevented from sailing out of Chatham by contrary winds. He went to Sheerness on New Year's Day, and then returned to London, indirectly confirming that Peter Peterson's testimony was false. On the next day he confesses to the Ordinary that with his trial looming he was persuaded to take desperate measures, including trying to get prosecution witnesses away from the Old Bailey by summoning them for invented debts.

The Ordinary concludes that Montgomery 'found himself surrounded on all sides with the greatest dangers, and plunged into a bad scheme, and the more he endeavoured to get out of it, the nearer he was to be swallowed up in it'.

Judith Defour

George Rudé notes that among the factors which made life for eighteenth-century London's lower classes 'hard, brutal and violent' was the struggle against 'wretched economic conditions'.[6] Surely, though, even a consideration of urban poverty does not prepare the mind for the impact of infanticide. The deliberate murder of children by their parents was the result of either shame or poverty; either the mother was unable to feed the additional mouth, or an illegitimate child might prove to be an insuperable obstacle to finding a situation in life.[7]

As London grew, it bred an underclass of people who had employment, yet were still very clearly in want. Rudé describes silk-weaving as 'one of the most chronically depressed of the skilled occupations of the day'.[8] Peter Linebaugh points to the poor pay earned by those in the weaving industry, but particularly the throwsters who twisted silk fibres to form thread. The master throwsters paid 'but small wages'.[9] The case of the Spitalfields throwster Judith Defour grimly shows how need could undermine maternal feelings.

At half past seven on the evening of 29 January 1734, Judith turns up for the night shift at the throwster's.[10] When she arrives, her friend Susan Jones asks her if she has taken her child back to the workhouse; Judith has permission to take her illegitimate daughter out for short periods of two or three hours before returning her to the parish workhouse where she is kept. No, Judith tells Susan; her mother has returned the child.

Judith works until one in the morning, and then she stops to have a dram, presumably of gin, an extremely cheap drink until duty is imposed under the 1736 Gin Act. She decides she'd like another, but Susan will not let her. Rather than return immediately to work, the impecunious Judith begs a penny to buy a roll and cheese. Susan gives her a penny and off she scuttles. When she returns, instead of a roll and cheese she brings back a roll and a halfpennyworth of gin.

She gets back to her work, but the gin seems to have loosened her tongue. Before long, she tells Susan, and Elizabeth Scot who is working nearby, that she has done something that deserves Newgate. Newgate Gaol being the traditional place for London's condemned to be held until taken to Tyburn to be hanged, Judith's meaning is clear. Susan says she hopes Judith has done nothing wrong to their employer, but that if she has her best way is to make a clean breast of it and confess, so that their mistress will be more inclined to look favourably on her. But Judith confesses that she has left her child in a field for the night.

'What?' cries Susan, 'In such a dismal cold night? How can you be so cruel?'

Judith backtracks and blames it on a woman called Sukey who she claims persuaded her to do it. Susan tells Elizabeth Scot to take a piece of bread and butter for the child, thinking she will be hungry as well as cold, and all three go straight to the field to fetch her. But Judith has not told them everything, and when they arrive they find the child stripped and lying dead in a ditch, with a linen rag tied hard about her neck.

Earlier that day, Judith took her daughter Mary from the Bethnal Green parish workhouse on Hare Street, near the parish church.[11] The child had been fathered by a weaver called John Cullender and was her second illegitimate child, the first having died in infancy.[12] She took little Mary and kept her until about six or seven in the evening, when she was with a woman called Susannah, whom she calls Sukey. Mary was wearing new clothes, given her by the workhouse a few days before, and Sukey pointed out to Judith that the clothes would fetch a good price.

Judith did not know Sukey well, not even knowing her surname; all Judith knew was that she had a sister in Shoreditch workhouse. Sukey persuaded Judith to sell the child's clothes. Since returning Mary to the workhouse would expose their scheme, Sukey persuaded her to carry little Mary into the fields and abandon her there. They took her to a field and stripped her, then they tied a linen rag very hard about her neck, apparently to prevent her crying out, but it strangled her.

Leaving Mary in a ditch, they went together to one Mary Witts, who lived in Swan Yard in the parish of St Leonard, Shoreditch. Sukey took charge and sold Mary's coat and stays for a shilling, and got four pence for the rest of the clothes. They shared the sixteen pence and then shared a quartern of gin. Later, after hearing of Judith's arrest, Sukey fled before she could be arrested.

When brought into court on 27 February 1734 and indicted for murder, Judith blames Sukey: 'that wicked creature Sukey seduced me to it'. Her mother, also called Judith Defour, says that her daughter 'never was in her right mind, but was always roving'. As the Ordinary of Newgate is at pains to point out later in the Ordinary's Account, her life has been an irregular one: he quotes her own confession that she had been 'always of a very surly disposition' as well as being 'negligent in her duty to God and man'. She was a drinker, 'delighting in the vilest companies and ready to practice the worst of actions'.

Judith is convicted of murder and sentenced to hang. She pleads her belly – in other words, she claims to be pregnant, which would spare her from the gallows – but a court of matrons is convened, a group of women whose duty it is to see whether there is any sign of a living child in the womb of the condemned woman. They conclude that there is not. Accordingly, Judith hangs at Tyburn on Friday 8 March. Of the seven people hanged that day, she is the only woman.

It is not only Judith's mother who believes that she has no proper understanding of right and wrong. The Ordinary's Account emphasises the pathos of the unnatural deed: he speaks of the helpless child in Judith's hands, 'smiling at the same Time in the Mother's Face, and calling out, Mammy; for she could speak no more'. However, he stresses that Judith had no teaching in right and wrong from her parents: 'She was very stupid and had little to say upon any Head'.

The evidence given at the trial by Jane Prig, of Bethnal Green Workhouse, would seem to confirm Judith's erratic character. When Judith arrives at the workhouse for Mary she has not bothered to get an order from the churchwarden, even though she must know the routine by now. Because Prig will not let her take Mary without one she goes away, waits for half an hour, and then comes back with a forged note. (Prig does not find out until later that it is forged.)

It is impossible to tell in what spirit Judith made her initial disclosure to her fellow workers at the throwster's, and from what is given it is difficult to assess her. The Ordinary's Account stresses her repentance according to her character, which gives a ring of authenticity. It is not a formulaic portrait. Indeed, her amoral upbringing and irresponsible sex life are advanced as illustrative of her character. She seems to be portrayed as a drifter, unwilling or unable to take control of her life. There is no doubt, however, that the murder of her child was prompted by poverty.

Joseph Lipman

As the Tower Hamlets became part of the burgeoning metropolis of London, poverty became more widespread as people crowded in until, as Henry Mayhew remarked pointedly in his preface to the 1861 edition of *London Labour and the London Poor*, London's poverty became 'to say the very least, a national disgrace to us'.[13] There was, however, no welfare provision at this time to help those forced to travel to seek employment. Thus when, in 1870, Joseph and Hannah Lipman have to travel to find work, they face a quandary. 13-year-old Joseph Junior is a boy with what these days are called special needs. A deaf mute, he has always been sickly and weak, and Hannah says he is more helpless than a baby. Her friend Rachel Harris will confirm in court that though Joseph is 13 years old, he does not look more than four or five. Also, he is so weak that he always has to be carried about; she has never seen him walk or even sit up, only lie.[14]

Joseph can eat anything large out of his hand, such as a slice of bread and butter, but he eats only bread and butter, potatoes, and fish. Sometimes though, he is so ill that he has to be fed with care. He suffers from diarrhoea at any sudden change in the weather, and when this happens he will go several days without being able to take food. From going without proper nourishment in this way he is always thin. Moreover, Hannah has to change his bedding often because of the state he is in. It is sometimes a bed of shavings, and sometimes of straw; it depends on what she can get.

Given the amount of care he requires, the Lipmans cannot take Joseph with them as they tour around in search of work, but what can they do with him? Presumably it is her husband who suggests that they should leave the boy with his brother Elias who has always been kind to Joseph, as Hannah will testify, and has treated him as if he were his own. Also, Elias and his wife have four children of their own, so they are used to childcare.

Elias and Mary Ann Lipman take in the boy. Whether or not they find the amount of care he requires difficult, the £3 15s they earn by doing so must have taken the edge off. Hannah pays them £2 15s up front, and writes to her friend Rachel to forward the other £1, which she does. Hannah and Joseph leave their boy very weak, as usual, but clean and in as good a state of general health as ever he enjoys. She also leaves a bath which is to be used for bathing young Joseph and some clothes.

Elias and Mary Ann live in the first-floor front room of 11 Boar's Head Yard, Whitechapel. They share this room with their four children and, at least from early July, a servant. Elias is a fishmonger, and is generally away from home. The servant, Hannah Sullivan, is with them for only three weeks, leaving because she doesn't get paid. She considers that the room is poorly furnished, and is presumably taken on because of the strain of looking after Joseph. Not that much care seems to be lavished on him.

On 24 July James Scott Sequira, a doctor living on Leman Street, is called to see to Joseph, he believes by the Lipmans (the message was left while he was out). When he arrives at Boar's Head Yard, only Mary Ann Lipman and a little boy are present. He notices Joseph is lying on some clothes in between a chest of drawers and a cupboard. The boy is emaciated, weak and prostrate. Turning up his shirt Sequira finds his body very dirty. His head is covered with old sores and scabs, and infested with vermin. He notices an abrasion of the skin on the left elbow, but no other marks other than the scabs on the head.

He asks Mary Ann what she has been feeding Joseph, and she says he had some milk not long previously. When he asks to see what she used to give him the milk she is unable to find it; presumably it has been washed up. Sequira orders that nourishment be given and he recommends medicine. He says also that Joseph ought to have been given wine.

This seems a curious suggestion to a present-day understanding, but Victorians had no problems with resorting to alcohol, and indeed stronger substances, to stimulate the weak. Moreover, their attitude to childhood was not so defined: it should be remembered that it was not until 1901 that child labour below the age of 12 was made illegal.

In court, Sequira cites Mary Ann as saying that 'she gave it a little wine yesterday, and it threw it up, and therefore it was of no use getting it, and that it was of no use getting other things, for he could not take them, or words to that effect'. There is surely more than a hint of despair in Mary Ann's attitude?

The information missing from the proceedings taunts the reader. Did Elias tell his wife what he was undertaking on their joint behalf? With four children to look after and a husband out of the home most of the time, Mary Ann must have been under considerable strain. Later, in court, Hannah Sullivan will testify to her mistress's attitude to the child, but this could be caused just as much by her despair as by cruelty.

At ten o'clock at night, PC Smith goes to 11 Boar's Head Yard because of 'information received'. Possibly the tip off came from Dr Sequira: Smith doesn't say. He has tried to get a relieving officer from the Poor Law Union to come with him. Mr Findlater, the relieving officer of Whitechapel, has refused to interfere because it is not in his district. Going to Mr Steddeford, the relieving officer of the proper district, Smith discovers that he is not at home.

When Smith enters the Lipmans' room, which he judges to be the usual kind of room occupied by the poor, he finds a gruesome sight. Lying on some rags, or possibly old clothes, in a small space between a cupboard and a chest of drawers in a corner of the room is Joseph Lipman, filthy, emaciated and seemingly very weak. There are bugs, lice and fleas on his body, and scabs on his head. Straight away Smith calls in the divisional surgeon, John Boynton Phillips, who arrives at about eleven o'clock.

The surgeon sees vermin running over Joseph's body from the rug. He sees lice on his body, and the whole surface of his skin is covered with dirt and with scales of skin which have been accumulating for a long time. Joseph's head is scabbed with old sores, and vermin are running over the scabs. Phillips judges that Joseph is dying from exhaustion. Mary Ann seems to have disappeared, as Phillips testifies later that there are only some children in the room. He cannot get any information from them.

What happens immediately after this is not recorded; by Wednesday however, Joseph is dead. His post mortem examination is carried out by Dr Phillips. He finds in the stomach just one or two teaspoons of some undigested thick fluid; none of it has passed into the intestines, so it can have been there only for a short time. The rest of the alimentary canal is empty, and the intestines are actually transparent, prompting the conclusion that no food has been given to Joseph for some time. Phillips concludes that the cause of death was chronic disease of the lungs and an ill-developed state of the nervous system, accelerated by starvation and general neglect.

Hannah Lipman is brought back to London. Whether from delicacy or some other motive is not made clear, but after the post mortem she is allowed to view only part of Joseph's face; she is not permitted to see his head.

On 15 August 1870, Elias and Mary Ann Lipman appear at the Old Bailey Sessions Court indicted for the manslaughter of Joseph Lipman. Telling evidence is given by their unpaid former servant Hannah Sullivan. She tells how when Mary Ann Lipman had her meals, she would give Joseph only a slice of bread and butter and a little water. Though largely he can eat by himself and does not need to be fed, still he gets virtually no food. Moreover, the bath Joseph's mother left for washing him was used by Mrs Lipman not to bathe Joseph, but to wash her clothes of a Friday. The only wash he gets is a wipe of the face with a flannel every morning.

Hannah tells how Joseph was made to sleep on a little bed with shavings and wood in it, and how his skin started to peel off with the hardness of the wood. She claims that she asked Mary Ann to go to a corn chandler's to get some straw for Joseph's bed; Mary Ann replied, 'B[ugge]r him, the little sod; let him die'. The details unveiled for the jury are grim and speak of harsh neglect, yet when they bring in a verdict of guilty of causing death by wilful neglect, they strongly recommend mercy. It would seem that the judge agrees; though indicted for manslaughter, Mary Ann Lipman is sentenced to just eighteen months' in prison.

Elias Lipman is found not guilty. Indeed, as far as the record goes no evidence is presented against Elias. Given that Hannah Lipman is so vocal in her assertion of his love for his sorely disadvantaged nephew, the question hangs over the proceedings: why did he do nothing? Is he not, as the legal head of the household, just as guilty of neglect? Moreover he does have a record: nine years previously he was given three months in prison for perverting the course of justice by helping a thief escape from a citizen's arrest. The thief had stolen the watch of a scripture reader called John King.[15]

Matilda Hewson

There are various illustrations of the grinding poverty which was besetting the area east of the City as the metropolis grew through the nineteenth century. The case of Elias and Mary Ann Lipman reveals also the dire state of housing in the East End: even though philanthropic housing ventures such as the Peabody Trust and the Improved Industrial Dwellings Company had been engaged in housing projects since the 1860s, most people were still living a family to a room like the Lipmans.[16] Such forced intimacy, however, could have grim consequences and seemingly, beneath the surface of the case of George Hewson and his daughter Matilda, there lurks a sinister secret.[17]

On Sunday 19 September 1847, Police Sergeant Joseph Price of H Division, Metropolitan Police, and PC William Day Davis of the City Police, are in Hackney Road when they see George John Hewson and his daughter Matilda, with Matilda's 3-year-old little boy. Davis has known Matilda for some time. She is visibly pregnant.

On the following Thursday, Matilda is with Frances Nathan, who lives with her husband Abraham in a ground floor room at 29 Sandys Row, Spitalfields. Their room is directly below that shared by Matilda

Hewson, her father George and the little boy. To Mrs Nathan, Matilda looks in good health, and is clearly far advanced in her pregnancy. However, on the Friday evening, at about eleven o'clock, Frances sees Matilda again, standing at the door and leaning against the frame. She now looks very ill. As Frances approaches, Matilda says to her, 'It is a fine night'. Frances agrees that it is, and then asks, 'Ain't you well?'

Frances replies, 'No, Mrs Nathan; I have got a cold'. She is still visibly pregnant.

As Friday evening gives way to Saturday morning, things start to happen, beginning with noises. At intervals from four o'clock in the morning, George Hewson is heard going downstairs and coming up again by Frances Nathan and Amelia Levy, who lives in the room next to the Hewsons on the first floor. Sometime after six o'clock Amelia Levy hears George knock at his door and call to Matilda, 'Are you asleep yet?' She answers, 'No'. Shortly she lets him into the room.

It is at about nine o'clock in the morning that Frances Nathan sees George Hewson from her window as he crosses the yard for the toilet, which is an open privy. He is carrying a pail, which she recognises as the one the Hewsons keep in their room. He is in the privy a minute or two and then he emerges, bringing the pail with him, and goes upstairs. A short time after this Frances herself goes to the privy, but as she crosses the yard she sees traces of blood on the ground.

Frances takes it on herself to wash the blood away; as she does, she sees Matilda Hewson looking down at her from the first-floor window. She calls up to her, 'Oh, Tilly, look at this; some person has been into the yard and done this. They ought to be ashamed to do so'.

Matilda replies, 'So they ought'. Frances turns back to washing away the stains and then goes back indoors, and so gives no evidence later as to Matilda's expression. Given what is to be disclosed, the reader of the trial record can infer sadness and, perhaps, regret in Matilda's answer, as she watches the trail of blood removed.

Between ten and eleven o'clock in the morning, shoemaker Patrick Curtain goes to the privy in the yard at 8 Rosetta Place, Spitalfields, where he lives with his wife and children. The yard in front of his home adjoins the backyard of 29 Sandys Row, and the privies are close together. As Curtain approaches the privy he is amazed to see the body of a baby boy lying on its right side, the head and mouth sunk in the putrid soil about two feet below the privy's seat. All he can see of the head is the left ear.

The baby has not been covered up completely, and what Curtain can see is quite clean, as if it has been washed. Curtain is not sure whether the child is alive, and he does not touch it; instead he calls for help. Mary M'Donald, who lives in the same house, comes out. She sees the baby, but she does not touch it either; nor does Bridget Curtain, Patrick's wife, who comes out just as M'Donald is going back in. Meanwhile, Curtain has gone for a policeman, stopping at 2 Frying Pan Alley to instruct John Josephs, a 'general dealer', to take the body of the child out of the privy.

It takes Josephs the best part of fifteen minutes to attend to the body. It is just as he is lifting the child from the soil that Curtain comes back, having been unable to find a policeman. From the yard at Rosetta Place, Curtain can see into the yard at 26 Sandys Row, where George Hewson is standing at the yard door. He can also see the window of the Hewsons' first-floor room, open at the bottom, and Matilda standing there looking out. She and her father watch on as Josephs lifts the limp body of the child from the foul, sticky soil. The child is cold. Josephs puts it into a tub of water to wash off the soil.

More people are gathering now, including Frances Nathan who sees Matilda at her window. Frances calls up to her, 'Curse that wretch – they are not ashamed to get them; and curse that wretch that would make away with them'. Matilda replies that it is a very great shame. Frances then remarks, 'It was no stranger,' to which Matilda replies that no, she does not think it was.

At around eleven o'clock, PC Henry Jowett of the City Police arrives. He lifts the child's body from the tub of water and wraps it in an apron which Mrs Curtain gives him. Jowett takes the body to a surgeon to pronounce the baby dead, and then to the dead-house at Christ Church, Spitalfields. Here the baby, still wrapped up in the apron, is locked in until it can be examined.

At about twelve noon or one o'clock, Frances Nathan goes into the Hewsons' room as Matilda is washing. She seems very ill; to Frances, a mother herself, Matilda looks 'like a lying-in woman'.

At about half-past nine on the next morning two policemen arrive: Sergeant Price and PC Davis, who both saw the Hewsons the previous Sunday on Hackney Road. Going into the first-floor back room they find George and Matilda, and the same little boy. There is very little furniture: there is one bed and a table, on which there are two glasses. There is a mattress on the floor, on which the boy lies. There are no clothes to be seen.

Matilda tells Price she has been ill, but has not been seen by a doctor. George Hewson tells him that Matilda has not been 'bodily ill'. At Matilda's request, Catherine Cronin is brought to see to her clothing before she is taken to the station. Catherine, a widow who lives in the same house, has known Matilda since she and her father came to Sandys Row, and some time ago she noticed that the girl was pregnant. When the men have withdrawn, Catherine says to her, 'Tilda, my dear, what is it you have done?' Matilda says nothing.

Catherine puts her arm under the younger woman's head to support her, since she seems rather faint. As she does so, Matilda looks up at her and begins to cry. Surely Catherine holds her close as she says, 'Tilda, my dear; I hope your father don't know anything about this'. In the depths of sorrow, Matilda replies, 'No, my father does not know anything about it'. This assertion that her father is ignorant of the situation becomes suggestive in the light of her later statements.

After a moment, Catherine changes Matilda's clothing, noticing that she is not as large as before, and that her bosom is full of milk. Catherine has had eight children herself, and to her Matilda appears like a woman who has recently given birth. But she says nothing about any child. Instead she says simply, 'Tilda, my dear; I am sorry for your misfortune'. Matilda gives no answer; she carries on crying.

Sergeant Price sends for a doctor; a Dr Thomas Mears examines Matilda, and though she denies the doctor's suggestion that she has recently borne a child, he finds on examination that she has. Price takes

George Hewson to the police station; he returns and he and Davis take Matilda to the station in a cab, from whence Davis takes her on to the Whitechapel Union Workhouse. As they are going to the workhouse, Matilda asks him what has been done with her father. Davis tells her that he has been locked up at the station.

'What for?'

'For secreting the birth of a male child that was found in the water-closet at the back of your house'.

Matilda rises to this, as much as she can. 'That is false, for my father knows nothing about it; he was out at the time the child was born, and he was out also when I put it down the water-closet'.

'Do you say that you did it?' Davis is uncertain how to take this. It is most unlikely, but then it is a confession and cannot be overlooked.

'Yes, it was me and not my father'. She tells him that the child was born about three days previously, in the evening.

'What time?'

'It was in the evening'. There is no other conversation. On arrival at the lying-in ward at the Whitechapel Workhouse, a nurse called Ellen Cochrane puts Matilda to bed.

Meanwhile, Thomas Mears has gone to the dead-house to examine the body of the child. He notes that it is a full-grown male baby and has been washed. There are no marks of violence about the child. The umbilical cord has been cut but not tied; nor has it been torn. The baby has passed his first stool, which would happen soon after birth, and shows he was born alive. Mears is unable to form a correct estimate of the time the child was born.

The next day, Ellen Cochrane hears Matilda say that on the previous Tuesday her father had left the house at nine o'clock in the morning and did not return until the evening. She says that during the day she gave birth to a little girl, and that there was no-one present in the room but herself and her little three year old boy. She claims that she herself took the child and put it down the water closet in the next yard; her father did not know anything of what happened until the Sunday. She says that she put the child down the water-closet the same day it was born. Two or three days afterwards, she says that it was her

113

father's cruelty and ill-usage that caused her to do what she did.

Leaving aside the unlikelihood that the child's body would not have been noticed in the privy between Tuesday and Saturday, what Matilda says is incorrect on two points. Her appearance in the days leading up to the Saturday, together with the noises heard that morning, suggest the baby was born in the early hours of Saturday morning. Moreover, she has the sex of the baby wrong, which makes no sense, unless she hardly saw the baby when it was born. Perhaps when the child arrived it was taken away by her father without her getting a good look at it; possibly this was to prevent her getting a chance to form an attachment.

Moving the day of birth from Saturday to a day when her father was absent seems to be her second attempt to exonerate him of involvement.

On 25 October 1847 Matilda Hewson and her father George John Hewson are indicted at the Old Bailey Sessions for infanticide, 'for the wilful murder of the new-born male child of the said Matilda Hewson'. George Hewson is found not guilty; Matilda is found guilty of concealing the birth, and is sentenced to eighteen months in gaol. However, George Hewson is convicted, on the same evidence, of unlawfully aiding and assisting Matilda in concealing the birth of the child. He is sentenced to two years' imprisonment.

Matilda's attempts to exonerate her father might have a darker motive than simple filial duty. This is suggested by a trial in the following year of one George John Hewson, admitted to Coldbath Fields House of Correction on 4 November 1847, ten days after the Hewson infanticide case opened at the Old Bailey Sessions. The closeness of the date and the similarity of the Christian names suggest that this is the same person. This George John Hewson is indicted at the Old Bailey on 3 July 1848 for the murder of William Henry Woodhouse, a warder at Coldbath Fields.[18]

The murder happened on Saturday 10 June 1848. At eight in the morning, Woodhouse brought Hewson before George Lavell Chesterton, Governor of Coldbath Fields. Hewson complained that he was being accused of, in the Governor's words, 'criminal intercourse with his own daughter, or something to that effect'. Hewson made the complaint to Woodhouse somewhere between half-past six and seven that morning, but rather than take the complaint seriously, Woodhouse said he would report Hewson to the Governor, to which Hewson replied, 'If you do, it will be the worse for you'.

At around half past eight, when the prisoners were having breakfast, Woodhouse went to Hewson's cell, where Hewson stabbed him. Crying out, 'Oh my God, he has stabbed me to the heart!' Woodhouse staggered back. Within three minutes, before he could be got out of the yard, he was dead. Hewson's comment on the killing was, 'Serve him right, a bloody villain!' He was placed in the personal charge of another warder, George Owen; that night and the following night he made a series of statements which Owen took down, having been instructed to do so by the Deputy-Governor. Owen recorded Hewson saying that 'at his trial he must mention circumstances that he is afraid will implicate his daughter with the disposal of two children'; shortly after this he said he hoped his daughter would not be brought to trial: 'if she is, there will be three separate cases to be heard'.

The possibility that Matilda, or her father, disposed of more than one child is bad enough. Given the nature of the taunting Hewson had received, it seems possible that Matilda conceived one or more children incestuously by her father. Such an unnatural intimacy must have been an ever-present danger, given the accommodation that the poor and lower paid were forced to endure before the advent of social housing.[19] It was usual for a family to have to live together in just one room, as they were doing at 29 Sandys Row. Moreover, George and Matilda lived alone together. Their only companion was a 3-year-old boy, whose parentage is not explained in the records, and who might therefore also be the result of incest.

Poverty stalked the East End in the nineteenth century, and often people were so dehumanised by need the usual conventions of human behaviour were overridden by more immediate necessities. It is this state of poverty that informs the usual vision of the East End. However, as has been seen, in the areas of eighteenth century commercial

115

development along the river and the edges of the City, desperate measures to escape debt were inspired by need.

The locations of these events have largely been swept away by later development. On the site of the Bethnal Green workhouse on Hare Street, now Cheshire Street, where Judith Defour's little daughter was kept, is the Great Eastern Railway's substantial goods depot, Reflection Works, built in the 1860s. Similarly, the site of the Whitechapel workhouse where Matilda Hewson was taken is now occupied by a block of flats called Lister House, while the sites of 29 Sandys Row and 8 Rosetta Place lie beneath the towering London campus of Newcastle University. Boar's Head Yard, in the sixteenth century the site of a Tudor theatre is, at time of writing, a derelict piece of ground on Whitechapel High Street to the west of Goulston Street.

Chapter 7

Recommended to Mercy

The concept of diminished responsibility did not enter British criminal law until the passing of the Homicide Act of 1957, which stated that a defendant shall not be convicted of murder 'if he was suffering from such abnormality of mind [...] as substantially impaired his mental responsibility for his acts and omissions in doing or being a party to the killing'.[1] Prior to this, the defendant's hope was to be recommended to mercy. The recommendation, which features at various points in this study, was made for a variety of reasons, and was not always successful.

The previous chapter saw the exigencies of poverty which inspired the recommendation to mercy of Mary Ann Lipman for the death of her nephew Joseph. This chapter explores three shootings which involved mitigating circumstances and show how fragile a hope the recommendation to mercy might be. They also reflect the domestic conditions of the late nineteenth century in the East End among the less poverty-stricken.

James Williams
The perils of the hothouse claustrophobia caused by multiple occupancy have surfaced in the previous chapter, which considered the pressures of poverty; yet multiple occupancy was not only a feature of the lives of the poor. Even in the later decades of the nineteenth century, much of the available housing often required a whole family to share a single room – each room hedged in by others just as densely occupied.

For someone suffering with what would easily be recognised as depression nowadays, this situation could prove intolerable. When, in the early hours of Thursday 3 December 1885, James Williams shot his sister Ellen, the tension had been building in the room since he came in drunk from the pub, but it was the proximity to another family that started the process that ended with the shooting.[2]

John Williams, a net-maker, lived with his son James and daughter Ellen in the first-floor back room at 8 Sheridan Street, St George's in the East, just to the north of Shadwell Station. The street no longer exists, having given way to development south of Watney Market, but was two streets north of Martha Street, which does survive. It was here that John and his son James worked making nets.

John Williams had been married twice, and had fathered nineteen children, but only three survived. Although all three children were living at Roberts Buildings, Commercial Road in 1883, within two years the family had divided. Joseph, the only child to survive from John's first marriage, ended up at 3 Queen's Buildings, Whitechapel, while John settled with his other two children at Sheridan Street.

At around twenty past twelve in the morning of 3 December, James Williams stumbles into the warmth of the shared room to find his father still up and waiting for him to come in. James is 18 years old. He has been a steady worker, a good support to his father and a loving brother to the 16-year-old Ellen. Also, since July that year, he has been a member of the Second Tower Hamlets Rifle Volunteers[3] and is making progress. Nevertheless, he has been drinking heavily of late, and is clearly drunk when he comes home. His father is still dressed, and though his sister has gone to bed, she is still awake.

James has been out since five o'clock. Around seven he met a friend called Frederick Matthews in a nearby pub; Matthews is a waterside labourer living in Haggerston, some miles to the north of Shadwell. James was not sober at seven, and when Matthews left him at half past eleven, he was completely drunk. Now he is home, all that matters to him is to get his father to go to bed.

'Are you waiting up for me, father?'

'No, Jimmy.' Of course he is; James was out much later than this on Monday night, and was out on Tuesday too. John Williams is starting to wonder what is happening to his son.

'Go to bed, father.'

'No, you go to bed.' James seems to accept this as reasonable, and begins to undress, but then he says again, 'You go to bed, father.'

Remembering that their landlord, Thomas Warby, hasn't come home yet, John goes down to check whether the drunken James has locked him out. Coming back he finds James undressed and writing something. The illiterate John is proud of his son's writing abilities, but surely it's a little late for this? James pauses in his writing to ask his sister, 'How do you spell Casen?' This is actually a loaded question and she replies, perhaps with a blush, 'Oh, you know better how to spell it, Jimmy, than I do.'

Suddenly James is alert. 'Hush! There is somebody in the passage.'

Although his father suggests that it is the landlord, James decides to check and makes his unsteady way downstairs in his shirtsleeves and goes out into the yard, witnessed by Warby, the landlord, as he takes a late supper. When he hears James climb back upstairs, Warby bolts the backyard door, then goes up to his own room, on the same floor as that of the Williams family.

Coming into the room James seems surprised to see his father still up; he asks again, 'Are you going to bed, father?' He is very drunk still, and is staggering.

'No, Jimmy, I am not going to bed yet.'

Resigning himself to his father's obstinacy, James turns back towards the door. Behind the door is his Volunteer's rifle. The Volunteers are not allowed to keep their weapons loaded. Before practice sessions their guns are examined, and when they've finished both the pouches and guns are examined. In this way the unit ensures that no Volunteer is permitted to take any ammunition away. But as James lifts the rifle, it goes off.

The shot hits his sister Ellen, who is still sitting up in bed. The post mortem examination will reveal that the bullet hits her right hand and travels along her right arm, shattering the bone; it is then deflected upwards and ploughs its way up the right side of her face, splintering the skull and driving fragments of bone into her brain. She loses consciousness immediately.

John Williams is on his feet. Crying out, 'Murder! Murder! You have killed your sister!' he grasps the gun. Calling out for Warby to come and help, John tries to wrestle the rifle away from James, but the boy is too strong. On entering the room Warby hears something of what James says as they struggle, something which explains why the boy was so insistent on his father's going to bed.

'I have shot my sister, I know I have shot her; and if you had been in bed as you were on Monday night I should have shot you first, and then Ellen, and then have done for myself.'

Warby manages to get possession of the rifle as John takes a cartridge from his son's left hand. It is a Martini Henry rifle: the cartridges are loaded and fired one at a time. Keeping hold of the rifle, Warby rushes out for a policeman; finding PC Thomas Bond, he explains what has happened as best he can, gives Bond the gun, and fetches him back to the house.

It is now about a quarter to one in the morning. Only twenty-five minutes have elapsed since James Williams came home from the pub.

Meanwhile, James has left the room and gone down to the floor below, to the room where John and Ellen Casen live. This is the name which he put to his sister earlier. Mr Casen comes to the door, and Mrs Casen is sufficiently awake to hear James ask him, 'Mr Casen, I have shot my sister; will you go for a constable and take me?' She must be wondering if she is dreaming, especially as James becomes aware of her and asks, 'Mrs Casen, I have shot my sister; will you go up to her?'

Ellen Casen rushes up to the still unconscious Ellen Williams, who is sitting up in bed, her face streaming with blood. Surreally she hears James come up after her and say to his father, 'Father, I owe Mrs Casen five shillings; take the bags home and pay her'. These are the bags on which he and his father have been working. He then goes outside the house to await the law, which is where PC Bond and Mr Warby find him.

James surrenders himself, saying, 'I throw myself in your hands; I have just shot my sister'. When shortly afterwards Bond asks him why he did it, James replies, 'I had a cause to do it. I meant to do it on

Monday. I brought three rounds from the butts; one I gave away and the others I kept. I did not like a letter that came here last Monday'. When Bond then tells him that he will be arrested and charged with attempted murder, James replies, 'I hope she is dead, and I will be hung for her.'

Later, Bond describes James as 'drunk and very excited', but his behaviour speaks more of resignation, as does his answer to Inspector John Quinn of H Division who arrives at about one o'clock. Quinn warns James, 'You will be charged with attempting to murder your sister and probably with murdering her'. James replies, 'Wilful murder; yes, I meant to do it'.

Meanwhile, the surgeon has arrived, a Mr Michael McCoy of 300 Commercial Road. After a preliminary examination of her wounds, Ellen is moved to London Hospital where McCoy will see her again, and where she will die later that morning at a quarter past eight, without having regained consciousness.

At the police station James is charged with attempting to murder his sister. He replies simply, 'Quite right, Governor'. When later that morning Quinn returns from the hospital to tell him that his sister has died and that he will be charged with murdering her, James replies, 'Yes sir'.

James Williams is committed to Clerkenwell House of Detention, where he is examined by the resident surgeon Llewellyn Morgan. All James can remember of the night in question is firing the rifle. Morgan visits him regularly, and then, on 7 December, James is seen at the prison by an eminent neurologist, Henry Charlton Bastian. Since 1867 he has been professor of pathology at University College London and assistant physician at University College Hospital; he has been assistant physician to the National Hospital for the Paralysed and Epileptic since 1868.

Charlton Bastian does not tell James that he is a medical man, nor why he is there. He spends nearly two hours with James, examining him about that night and asking questions with a view to testing his mind. Bastian asks James, 'Do you recollect loading the rifle?' James

121

replies that the rifle was not loaded and was never kept loaded. Bastian then asks, 'Don't you recollect about the report?' James replies that he remembers firing the rifle and hearing his sister scream.

Charlton Bastian finds no evidence that James is not of sound mind.

His plan to shoot his father and sister dead and then kill himself is not James Williams' first attempt at suicide. Nearly two years previously, on 26 December 1883, James shook hands with one Sarah Isaacs, who had known him all his life, and said to her, 'Good-bye, you will never see me again'. She tried to make a joke of this: 'Oh yes I shall, if I only see your body'. Later that evening, PC H311 Henry Brown saw James with five or six others coming over Old Gravel Lane Bridge in Wapping. Spanning the waterway connecting two parts of London Docks – Tobacco Dock and the Eastern Dock – it was a known suicide spot.[4] Moments later, James was in the freezing water; it looked like he could swim but was out of his depth. He was also drunk, increasing the danger of hypothermia. It was about nine o'clock, and very dark.

PC Brown threw James a rope and pulled him out. He took the sodden, shivering boy back to the station and charged him with drunkenness and attempted suicide; subsequently James was fined half-a-crown for drunkenness. Why, on Boxing Day, would a teenage boy, among a crowd of friends, want to drown himself in the docks? The answer is a girl.

Sarah Isaacs, whose hand James shook earlier that day, had a girl in her service at her house at 25 Cecil Street, off of Commercial Road. We do not learn the girl's name, but she died earlier in 1883. The sixteen year old James was attached to the girl, and may have been engaged to her. Looking back while testifying in court in 1885, his half-brother Joseph remembers the change brought about in James by her death: 'he said that he wished he was after her; he would be dead soon'. Similarly, their father testifies in court that people have pointed out the change to him, and that he has noticed it himself.

The effect of the young girl's death on James was deep-rooted and coloured his attitude to his sister Ellen's developing relationship with James Maloney. A private in the First Battalion of the West Surrey

Regiment, he was also the brother of the above-mentioned Ellen Casen and would visit the house quite openly in uniform. At some point during those visits he got to know Ellen Williams. Clearly they got on; they began to 'walk about', and twice he took her out. But on 17 November 1885 James Maloney was posted to Cork. Before he left for Ireland, Ellen asked him to write to her, which he did on 21 and 28 November.

Rather than be happy for his sister, it would seem that James became morbidly jealous. He began to drink heavily. His drinking friend Frederick Matthews confirmed that James took to drinking spirits rather than beer and that 'the stuff got very quickly up to his head'. The two were drinking into the night on the Monday, Tuesday and Wednesday evenings before the shooting.

At about two o'clock on the Tuesday morning, having drunk through Monday evening, they found themselves crossing London Bridge. When they were about midway across, James ran suddenly away to the parapet and tried to get up onto it. Thankfully Matthews was able to grab James and pull him down, but he made a second rush for the river and had to be pulled back down again.

This extreme behaviour seems to have stemmed from one of Private Maloney's letters from Cork. After shooting his sister, James confessed to PC Bond that he did it because 'I did not like a letter that came here last Monday'. The letter arrived on 1 December addressed to Ellen Williams, but was picked up by John who, though unable to read, recognised the name 'Williams'. Thinking it an order for work, he gave it to James. As he read it to himself, his father asked, 'Jimmy, who is it from?' James replied, 'It is not for you, it is from Cork'. At this, Ellen sat up in bed and claimed her letter, and John took it from his son.

That drink caused his resentment to fester is supported by statements at his trial from the medical experts who assessed James. Llewellyn Morgan, the surgeon at Clerkenwell, testifies that a little beer would upset James' brain; George Henry Savage, medical superintendent of Bethlehem Hospital, believes that 'excess of drink would probably disturb him rapidly and unduly'. Additionally, the medical experts conclude that James has a lower than average mental capacity.

Charlton Bastian judges that James is 'of a distinctly low mental type and probably not a very strong brain'; Savage believes that though not 'actively insane' James is 'of a low intellectual power'.

It is to the operation of drink on his mind that they attribute James' claims to having seen visions. Charlton Bastian tells the court that James claimed people came into his cell, and that he saw two friends playing at bagatelle in his cell one night. Savage reports that James said he had seen men's faces at night. It is not only the experts who have heard of James's visions however. In court Sarah Isaacs tells how, after her maid's death, he told her that he saw 'such a lot of men come into his room to trouble him'.

John Williams also testifies that James told him that he had seen people coming into his room and worrying him. His father's unhelpful response to these admissions was to laugh at him. Though it may well have been the drink that caused the visions, it could possibly have been some deeper instability: John says that James would mention these visitors 'worrying him' sometimes after bouts of drinking, but also sometimes 'before he had had any drink'.

There is no record of a recommendation to mercy at the trial, but though indicted for, and charged with, the wilful murder of his sister Ellen Williams, James was found guilty of the lesser charge of manslaughter, and sentenced to fifteen years' imprisonment.

William Redhead

James Williams was not the only rifleman with the Tower Hamlets Volunteers to have been driven to commit murder by his domestic situation. Some years previously, on 30 May 1870, William Redhead shot dead his stepmother Sarah at their home, 80 Sidney Street. Though the house no longer exists, there are surviving examples at the same end of the street which give an idea of what the address looked like. However, while James Williams was upset emotionally, William Redhead was the victim of domestic provocation.[5]

Sometime after two o'clock in the afternoon of Monday 30 May 1870, Mrs Ann Brighton is cleaning a pail in the yard of 80 Sidney Street where she and her husband rent a room. The landlady, Sarah Redhead, comes out into the yard while she is doing this, and spends about five minutes chatting with her before going indoors. Mrs Redhead then goes up to the first floor to chat with Mrs Mary Ann Morris who, with her husband, is another of the tenants. Mrs Morris is washing some dishes.

While Mrs Redhead is chatting with Mrs Morris there is a knock at the front door, so she breaks off to go down and answer it. Just as she is turning the bend in the staircase, a gunshot rips the silence and Sarah Redhead drops down dead. Shot from below, the bullet passed through her body and lodged in the wall, breaking the tenth rib and lacerating her heart as it went. Death must have been instantaneous.

At the sound of the shot, Mrs Morris rushes to the landing to look, but as the smoke reaches her face she is overcome with fear. Running back into her room she locks the door behind her, rushes to the window and screams for help. Meanwhile, Mrs Brighton has heard the shot through the open back door and has rushed in just in time to hear the front door being shut. In the passage she sees Sarah Redhead lying at the bottom of the stairs; her face is to the stairs, and her feet point to the door of the back parlour, the room occupied by her stepson William.

Mrs Brighton runs out to the backyard, then, seeing no-one there, she rushes through the house, opens the front door and, once outside, shouts for help, her cries mingling with those of Mrs Morris upstairs.

John Newell, a local grocer at 106 Oxford Street (nowadays Stepney Way) is standing at his door when he hears the gunshot and sees William Redhead shut the door and leave. At the same time Thomas Ashton, a tailor at work on the first floor at 83 Sidney Street, exactly opposite number 80, hears the shot. As he looks out of the window, he sees William run out, carrying his rifle and looking very excited.

William pulls the door to, turns to his left and heads off towards Mile End Road at a sort of sling-trot, a half-march, half-run used by soldiers primarily for covering rough terrain. He is, therefore, not running particularly fast. Ashton loses sight of him when he takes the second turning on the right, possibly Robert Street (which has long since disappeared). He is not making much of an effort to get away; indeed, he is actually seeking arrest.

He covers the best part of a mile before he sees PC K356 William Smith on Alfred Street (nowadays Shandy Street). Smith doesn't notice William until he approaches and speaks to him, saying, 'Now I have done it'. William is still carrying his rifle. PC Smith is presumably a little nonplussed; no doubt he is not usually approached by rifle-carrying young men. He asks William what he has done; William replies, 'I have shot my mother in-law'.

'Where?'

'At 80 Sidney Street, and after I did it I set fire to the house, and I mean to give myself up to you.'

William, it transpires, had also set fire to his room before leaving the house; presumably just before shooting his stepmother since Mrs Brighton heard the door close. This piece of arson is problematic. Since William is not seeking to escape, clearly he is not seeking to cover his flight. Perhaps he is trying to get rid of the house because of its associations with the stepmother he has just put out of the way?

Back in Sidney Street, the shouting has attracted a crowd, and from his window Thomas Ashton sees Sarah Redhead being carried out of the house by a group of neighbours who put her into a cart to be taken to the nearby London Hospital. But they are prevented by the arrival of the local doctor, Robert Swyer, from Mile End Road. He has Sarah taken back indoors, in the hope that he can do something to resuscitate her. She has no pulse and all he can do is to strip and examine the body.

The positioning of the wounds allows Swyer to deduce where the police should look for the bullet. PC K346 William Turney has been examining the premises, and he locates the ball about halfway up the staircase, embedded about two inches into the wall, and he digs it out. Meanwhile, Swyer tries to look at William's room but cannot get in because William has set it on fire: he manages to look in, but then has to close the door.

In the meantime PC Smith, having taken William to the police station at Arbour Road, has been reporting to Sergeant Edward Dillon. Dillon lays the rifle on one side in the charge room, and then charges William with the wilful murder of his stepmother by shooting her through the body with a loaded rifle. All William says in reply to this is, 'Yes, I did it'.

In Dillon's presence, Smith searches William and finds five ball cartridges and six caps. He watches Sergeant Dillon examine the rifle; on the nipple Dillon finds a cap which appears to have been fired recently. The caps and the cartridges Smith has found fit the rifle. Dillon points this out; William replies, 'Yes, they are mine; I am a rifleman'. Later in court, Sergeant Page of the Tower Hamlets Volunteers will confirm that the cartridges are similar to those served out by him for practice, and that they are standard caps.

Sergeant Dillon writes down the charge in the charge-sheet and reads it out to William. Then Police Superintendent Edward Worrall of K Division asks William if he has anything to say in answer to the charge, warning him that what he does say will be taken down in writing. William says, 'All that I have to say is that she was very unkind to me and my sister; that is all I have to say'.[6]

Worrall writes this down, and then he adds a note to say that 'I asked the prisoner if he had anything to say in answer to the charge'. William is looking at Worrall all the time he writes, and a number of other witnesses see it also.

On 11 July William Redhead is indicted at the Old Bailey Sessions for the wilful murder of Sarah Redhead. It is made clear that the shooting was carefully planned. After all, William has been a member of the Seventh Tower Hamlets Volunteer Rifles for five months now, and has been thoroughly trained in the use of a rifle. Indeed, Sergeant Page confirms that he has been trying to get recognition for his skills, and two days prior to the murder he was firing at the range to try and get his second-class accreditation, which would allow him to progress to first class. He failed to get it.

During the trial Dr Swyer is asked to give his opinion on how the shooting must have been carried out, based on how the wounds were inflicted. He has some experience of firearms, as well as an acquaintance with William Redhead, since he is the surgeon to the Seventh Tower Hamlets Volunteer Rifles. His opinion is that the rifle must have been levelled in readiness before Sarah Redhead appeared, and fired just as she came into sight. She was shot before she had a chance to turn the bend in the stairs; if she had got as far as the bend, she would have been shot from in front.

The killing was premeditated, but how responsible for his actions was William Redhead? Like James Williams, he had a sister called Ellen. For some reason she does not feature in his trial at the Old Bailey, but she was at the inquest held on 2 June 1870, and the following day's *Glasgow Daily Herald* reports that she testified at the inquest to their stepmother's cruelty towards William.[7] Moreover, *The Herald* records that when the jury returned a verdict of wilful murder, an application was made to the coroner that the killing be considered to be manslaughter. However, Coroner Humphreys ruled that as the crime was not committed in the heat of passion it was a murder.

According to *The Teesdale Mercury* of Wednesday 8 June 1870, enquiries showed that 'the marriage of the prisoner's father to a second wife gave much offence to his children by his first wife, and they lived on very bad terms'.[8] The *Mercury* summarises the pressures suffered by William at home, including Sarah pawning his clothes to get money for drink. It further states that he had 'for some time led a very unhappy life, owing to the tyranny of the woman whose life he has taken in the wild spirit of revenge' and records his confession to friends that he was 'so miserable that he was afraid he should kill her some day or other or drown himself'.

With their father away much of the time as a ship's steward, William and Ellen Redhead will not have had much relief from their stepmother's company. It is likely that resentment was building, and William's failure the previous Saturday to secure his badly wanted second-class accreditation at target shooting can have done nothing to cheer him up. Sergeant Page testifies at the inquest and at the trial that on the Saturday, William seemed 'rather low-spirited'; perhaps seeing not only his progress as a rifleman but also the 10s grant elude his grasp may have been sufficient to provoke him to act.

The *Mercury* describes Redhead as 'a quiet-looking lad, without any indication of ferocity in his countenance or demeanour'. Mary Ann Morris testifies at his trial that William has been regular in his work habits, and this is borne out by the fact that, of the eight character witnesses who speak for him at the trial, seven are from the firm of wine merchants that employed him. Sergeant Page bears witness that William has been very regular at his drill throughout his time with the Volunteers. He adds that William was 'always exceedingly quiet and well behaved' and that his instructing sergeant was very satisfied with him.

The jury are clearly attuned to William Redhead's situation, and when they bring in the inevitable verdict of guilty, nevertheless they recommend him to mercy 'on account of his youth and good character'. The recommendation is not taken up, and the sentence of death is passed. However, this is commuted subsequently to one of life imprisonment.

At the Williams trial, Sergeant Major Marley of the Second Tower Hamlets Rifle Volunteers was at pains to point out the impossibility of smuggling out ammunition from the practice range. Nevertheless both James Williams and William Redhead shot their victims with their Volunteer's rifles. Both killings were clearly premeditated. It is significant though that both William Redhead and James Williams surrendered themselves for arrest. Moreover, the shootings were carried out in crowded houses, with a cast of witnesses on hand to testify in court. There is nothing covert at all about these crimes, which were the results of sheer despair.

John Parr

It is noteworthy that although William Redhead was recommended to mercy by the jury, he was denied it to begin with; his death sentence was only commuted to one of imprisonment later. There was never a guarantee that mercy would be shown through compassion for the defendant's state of mind. Perhaps it was because of his occupation as a petty criminal that compassion was withheld from John Parr when charged with the murder of his fiancée in the centenary year of 1900.[9]

On the evening of Saturday 25 August 1900, three young women are out in Shoreditch when they are approached by the 19-year-old John Parr. He knows two of them, Caroline Potter and Winifred Clark, but this is the first time he has met Winifred's sister Lily. Parr takes them into a pub called *The Horns* at 1 Hackney Road across from St Leonard's church. Being a Saturday evening, the pub is doing good business.

As will be testified later at his trial, Parr has a vain and bombastic way about him, and no doubt he relishes being the centre of attention. In the pub, he takes out a photograph and shows it to the women. It is a picture of Caroline's 19-year-old sister Sarah Willett, Parr's fiancée (spelled Willott in the Proceedings). Perhaps with some gravity, he tells the women that he has been thinking of her while he has been away. He kisses the photograph and puts it back into his pocket. But then he says something that must surely make an impression: he tells them that he intends to kill Sarah and then himself.

Though there are other people in the bar, Lily Clark thinks no-one else hears this. None of the women recall him saying anything more, or offering an explanation, so presumably Parr then continues to drink without further comment. It is possible he leaves the comment hanging deliberately for effect, because Parr has not yet finished his performance.

When they leave the pub and head south to Bethnal Green, Parr brings out a revolver and, aiming up into the air, he fires. All three women are, of course, startled at the sound of the shot, and Caroline remembers screaming, but Winifred asks for a bullet from the gun. Parr opens the chamber and gives one of the unspent bullets to her and one to Caroline. Lily is in front and presumably she is keeping her face forwards, because she says afterwards that she did not see this; maybe she is reluctant to be impressed by this strange young man?

Parr mentions to the women that he has been having a quarrel with his fiancée because she has been going with other men while he has been away. 'Instead of hearing of a marriage,' he says ominously, 'you will hear of a funeral'. Though Lily will claim in court that she doesn't take what he has said seriously, nevertheless she warns Sarah the next day, as does Winifred.

The following afternoon, Parr comes across his fiancée Sarah in Victoria Park with her friend Emily Sampson. Sarah and Parr talk together, but all Emily hears is Parr asking, 'Where are you going?' and her answer, 'For a walk'. To this he says, 'So am I', and he follows them from the park all the way to the door of the place where they are both living. Here, Sarah stands and speaks to Parr; Emily stands to one side until he leaves, unable to tell whether or not it is a friendly conversation.

The next day, Monday 27 August, at about 9.20 pm, Sarah and Emily are together at the Foresters Music Hall on Cambridge Road (now Cambridge Heath Road), Mile End. Now demolished, it was a prestigious venue, where the likes of Dan Leno, Little Titch and Charlie Chaplin himself made their debuts,[10] and no doubt the bill of fare is a good one. But this is spoiled somewhat by the arrival of John Parr.

He comes to where they are watching the performance and speaks to Sarah. Again, Emily cannot hear what is being said, but then Sarah takes her into the bar to have a drink; Parr follows. He asks Sarah to treat him and when she says no, he picks up her glass of stout and drinks it. At this Sarah says, 'Come outside, Emma'.

They go out into the Cambridge Road and head north. As they walk, Parr walks uninvited by Sarah's side; Emily is on her other side. As they walk, Parr asks Sarah if she will have a drink; again she says no. Turning left into Bethnal Green Road, Sarah stops outside the police station and asks Parr, 'What do you intend to do?' He replies, 'I intend to have you, and no one else'. Sarah's last words are, 'I don't want you; all I want is an honest, hard-working fellow, not one who robs others'. She then turns round and without another word goes up the police station steps, holding Emily by the arm.

As they go, Parr pulls out his revolver and, as he follows the two women up the steps, he fires at Sarah. Emily sees the flash of the shot and hears Sarah scream and fall. Police Sergeant George Crow also hears the shot and emerges from the station, followed by PC Richard Wood; he sees Parr on the steps, revolver in his hand. Crow and Wood seize him and take him into the station. Meanwhile Sarah is carried in by two more policemen, with Emily following; she is unconscious, and dies some three or four minutes later.

Having got Parr inside, Crow takes the gun from him and gives it to Inspector William Page, who is in charge of the station. Crow hears Parr say, 'I have done it; I have done it'. Page inspects the five-chambered revolver. It contains five cartridges: four are loaded and one has been discharged recently. Subsequently he charges Parr with the wilful murder of Sarah Willett; Parr makes no reply. He is placed in the charge of PC Wood, who searches him and finds a small pocket book containing a photograph of Sarah and a piece of paper. On the paper is written, 'It is all her own fault, and she deserves it. Good-bye pals, one and all'. Later in court Parr will claim that he intended to commit suicide after killing Sarah, and this would seem to indicate that.

Local doctor John David Jenkins MD arrives at the police station to see Sarah Willett's body. He finds on her right temple a more or less circular wound from which some blood-stained brain matter protrudes. There is no exit wound, and three days later the post mortem will reveal the bullet still lodged in her brain. Jenkins also sees Parr, who is in a dazed condition and does not seem to understand what is being said to him. Jenkins has never before seen a man immediately after a murder, so he judges that there is nothing unusual about Parr's state of mind, considering what has just happened. Jenkins does not ask Parr anything beyond his name, and examines his tongue to make sure he is not unwell.

On the next day, 28 August, Caroline Potter hands in the cartridge Parr had given her to Sergeant Crow. On the same day, Parr is remanded to Holloway Prison, where he is seen by the medical officer, Dr James Scott, and placed in the infirmary to be kept under close observation, Scott's usual practice in cases such as this. His initial impression is that Parr is rational and coherent in his conversation, though he judges his intellect to be of a somewhat low order. When he asks Parr if there are any traces of insanity in his family he can get nothing from him. However, Scott finds in his conversation traces of vanity and bombastic talk; he notices it particularly when Parr doesn't know he's being observed.

Two days later, as Dr Jenkins makes his post mortem examination, George William Hood, assistant warder at Holloway, sees Parr writing a letter. It is to Sarah Willett, mother of the victim, who receives it in the post the next day. In it Parr asks how she is. He says that what has happened was a great blow, but that it was not his fault. He claims that nothing would have happened if the younger Sarah had said one word to him. All would have been well, but her temper would not allow her to speak to him. He says he will be at the inquest, and that he hopes to see her there. He asks her to bear up for the sake of the little ones, whose names he has forgotten.

A mystery overhanging the John Parr trial is his supposed trip to Australia earlier that year to visit a cousin. He had told the elder Sarah Willett that he was going that same night, intending to come home just before Christmas. He was still in London on the following day however, when he told his mother Emma Parr he was leaving; he said good-bye to her and then went out, taking a portmanteau with him.

Given that it took some thirty-five to forty days to steam from Britain to Australia in 1900, he would have needed ten weeks for the speediest journey there and back, which does not account for any time spent out there. According to his mother he was away for only six weeks. When he reappeared, he did not return home; his mother didn't know where he was, and the next she saw of him was at Worship Street Police Station.

Both his mother and Sarah's mother noticed that, when he declared he was going away, his behaviour had been erratic. While having a drink with Mrs Willett he had had a fit; gradually falling from his chair on to the floor, and had taken ten minutes or so to bring him round. Back home later that evening, he threw himself across the table in front of his mother and would not tell her what the matter was. On the following day he was glaring and appeared agitated.

His strange behaviour at that time was not an isolated incident. In court, Emma Parr tells of his fits when he was a baby; though they stopped after a time, they seemed now to be recurring. Mrs Willett testifies that there was something strange in his manner at times, and that he seemed to be dazed and worried, as if he had something on his mind. His brother George tells that he 'would walk about in a lonely way; he seemed low-spirited and moody; he had said very strange things'. George also says that their mother told him that Parr would shave his arms and legs and pose in front of a mirror like a statue. She recounts how she had told him that she should 'get someone in to look after him'.

It comes out at the trial that there are incidents of insanity in his family. His mother has a brother who has spent time in Colney Hatch Asylum, the largest and most modern psychiatric hospital in Europe when it opened in 1851. On his father's side there are three more cases of insanity, two of whom have also been through Colney Hatch. Moreover, any inherited mental health issues may well have been affected by a head injury he had some years before.

This is mentioned at the trial by both Sarah Willett and George Parr, the latter confirming 'I have noticed a change in his manner since', but his mother is more explicit. Emma Parr testifies that, after having a fall in the gymnasium, he 'seemed changed in his manner'. His hair fell out, and he 'would pull and tear things in an agitated manner'. She took him to the doctor and he received treatment for four or five weeks. She testifies that subsequently he had headaches and would bleed from his nose and ears.

The medical witnesses, however, do not consider that Parr might be insane. John Jenkins, the surgeon called to the police station, believes that Parr behaved as he did because he had shot someone: 'I should not expect him to be quite calm and collected'. James Scott, the medical officer at Holloway, maintains that his examinations yielded nothing suggestive of insanity, even though he has heard of the instances of insanity in Parr's family and has drawn attention in court to Parr's vanity and bombastic talk, which Scott claims to be indicators of an unsound mind. Similarly, Brian Block and John Hostettler in *Hanging in the Balance: A History of the Abolition of Capital Punishment in Britain,* comment on the hanging of Joseph Holden at Strangeways prison in Manchester in December 1900, that: 'his sanity had been in some doubt, but was 'affirmed by medical opinion".[11]

At the end of the trial, and in the face of such testimony, the jury enter a strong recommendation for mercy, but this is 'on account of his youth'. John Parr receives no mercy. While he would seem to be a prime example of a case of diminished responsibility, perhaps it is his criminal life as a thief which prevents him receiving mercy. This hovers, barely acknowledged, behind the record of his trial. Sarah Willett's retort that she wanted 'an honest, hard-working fellow, not one who robs others' speaks of this darker side to his life, as does his possession of a revolver. There is also his mysterious absence, which he claimed was a visit to Australia though such a journey could not be done in the time. Was he on a job elsewhere?

Whatever the reason for his receiving no mercy, on Tuesday 2 October 1900, John Parr is hanged in the execution shed at Newgate Gaol. According to Brian Block and John Hostettler, Parr 'left no statement and expressed no contrition'.[12]

There are similarities between the shooting of Sarah Willett and the shootings of Ellen Williams and Sarah Redhead. It is a far from covert affair and, as with James Williams, it seems that John Parr had intended to commit suicide: at his trial he said he had meant to shoot himself the night before, and a seeming suicide note was found in his pocket. Like James Williams, a fiancée was involved, though James did not shoot her. John Parr, however, was a different kind of character from James Williams.

There are reminders surviving of John Parr's story: *The Horns* public house still stands, though now it is a strip club called *Brown's*. The former police station still stands on Bethnal Green Road, occupied by the Providence Row Housing Association; the steps are not those on which he shot Sarah Willett however, as the building was refaced when it was extended in 1917. Sadly, Foresters Music Hall no longer survives. It closed in 1917 and stood decaying until it was demolished in 1965.[13]

Chapter 8

The City's Violent Shadow

With the discovery of the body of Mary Ann Nichols in the early hours of the morning of Friday 31 August 1888, a dark legend began to grow which has come to dominate criminal history. The story of Jack the Ripper seems to sum up everything that was dark about the streets of Whitechapel and Spitalfields in the later decades of the nineteenth century; so much so that 'Ripperologists' seem to be ever on the lookout to identify new victims, and many murders or attempted murders are included one way or another in the 'butcher's bill'.

Possibly the greatest mystery about the murders committed by Jack the Ripper is why they dominate our collective imagination. There have, after all, been far worse and more sinister serial killers since the autumn of 1888; moreover, the actual murders of the five 'canonical' victims are actually quite straightforward, the cause of death being a cut throat; the gruesome mutilations were carried out after death. Perhaps it is the continual speculation about the identity – and even the gender – of the killer which generates the interest. Had he (or she) been caught and hanged, perhaps the mystery would have dissipated, of interest only to criminologists and psychologists. Perhaps of greater significance is the climate of violence at the time, within which the Ripper appears as a startling but not too outstanding criminal.

Emma Smith and Martha Tabram
In April 1888, Emma Elizabeth Smith, a 45-year-old widow, had been living for eighteen months in a common lodging house at 18 George Street, Spitalfields. Emma was a prostitute, but she hinted at having come down in life. The word was that Emma had come to London from the country, and had not seen any of her friends for ten years. The common lodging houses of the East End were of highly dubious

character, and used by the extremely poor; usually each room contained a number of single beds, rented by the night for three or four pence.

The common lodging houses were rightly infamous. They were grim places to find shelter, as William Fishman notes: 'The most horrific conditions were attributed to those lodging houses catering for the casual poor'.[1] The terrible conditions of the lodging houses were not their only drawback. Mostly the houses were used by prostitutes, and contained double beds for their use: indeed, Fishman describes the 'lower doss' as operating usually as 'an open working-mart for prostitutes'.[2]

Just how widespread the dubious reputation of the common lodging houses was, becomes apparent in the statement made in court by one Susannah Palmer, as she justified attempting to murder her reprobate husband James on 19 December 1868: 'there is not a lodging-house in Whitechapel that he has not been turned out of'.[3] Mrs Palmer, who lived with her costermonger husband at Grasshopper Court, near Old Street, was found guilty of wounding feloniously, but the jury 'strongly recommended her to mercy in consequence of the great provocation she received'. Her sentence was respited.

At about seven o'clock in the evening of 2 April 1888, Easter Bank Holiday Monday, Emma Smith goes out, as witnessed by Mrs Mary Russell, deputy keeper of the lodging house. She also sees Emma return between four and five in the morning, badly beaten, with blood everywhere. Her face and head have gruesome injuries, and her right ear hangs down, having been nearly torn off.[4]

Emma says she has been set upon and robbed of all her money; she also complains of pains in her abdomen. Mary hurries her to the nearby London Hospital. On the way they turn from Wentworth Street onto Osborn Street, and Emma points out the spot where she was assaulted. She says there were two or three men, but is unable to describe them; she believes that one of them was about 19 years old.

It is clear that between her leaving George Street and coming back Emma was touting for trade. Margaret Hayes, another resident of 18

George Street, saw Emma at Limehouse in the early hours of the morning of Tuesday 3 April. Margaret was hurrying away from the area, having been smacked in the mouth when accosted by some young men, and saw Emma across the road at the corner of Farrant Street and Burdett Road. She had a man with her of about medium height, and Margaret noted his dark clothes and white silk neckerchief. Not a cheap prospect then: perhaps someone from up West slumming it in the East.

What happened to Emma next is gleaned only from her statements while still conscious. By about half past one she was back in Whitechapel, passing the church of St Mary Matfelon, the White Chapel which gave the area its name, but was demolished after the Second World War. Seeing some men approaching, she crossed Whitechapel Road and headed up Osborn Street. Seemingly they followed her because as she reached the Wentworth Street turning, by the Taylor Brothers chocolate and mustard factory, they caught up with her, beat her up and robbed her.

The beating was particularly savage, far more so than would be expected of street robbery, but that was not the worst of it. One of her attackers used a blunt instrument – perhaps his cudgel – to object-rape her, pushing it so forcefully into her that it ruptured her peritoneum, the lining of the abdomen. Then they fled the scene, leaving Emma to try and orient herself and make her slow, painful way home.

At the hospital Emma is seen by George Haslip, the duty surgeon. She is still bleeding from the head and ear, and on examination he sees that she has other injuries, which he describes later as 'of a revolting nature'. She tells him she cannot say what kind of instrument was used on her, and shortly after this she slips into a coma; she does not regain consciousness, and is pronounced dead at nine o'clock the following morning. The post mortem examination conducted by Haslip reveals that Emma's organs are generally normal; he has no doubt that death was caused by injuries to the perineum, the abdomen and the peritoneum. He concludes that great force must have been used, and that the injuries caused peritonitis which resulted in her death.

The inquest is held on Saturday 7 April, at London Hospital, before

Wynne Edwin Baxter, Coroner for East Middlesex, who later will preside over the inquests of the first three 'canonical' victims of Jack the Ripper: Mary Ann Nichols, Annie Chapman and Elizabeth Stride. Emma Smith's inquest is short; it takes only one day. Saying that he considers it 'impossible to imagine a more brutal and dastardly assault', Coroner Baxter advises the jury that it would help the interests of justice if a verdict might be given, rather than adjourning the inquest. Accordingly a verdict is recorded of wilful murder, against person or persons unknown.

The person or persons remain unknown, as does the murderer of Martha Tabram, who lived for a time at the lodging house next door to Emma Smith's, at 19 George Street. Also a prostitute, Martha was last seen on a Bank Holiday, like Emma, but this time it was Monday 6 August 1888. She seems to have died at the place where she was attacked, on the stairs of George Yard Buildings, erected in 1875 to provide accommodation for the poor.[5] It has been demolished, but George Yard itself survives as Gunthorpe Street, leading north from Whitechapel High Street.

Martha was found at around a quarter to five in the morning of 7 August by John Reeves of 37 George Yard Buildings, on his way to work. In fact, she was found first by cabbie Albert Crow of Number 35 who was just coming off shift, but when, at half past three, he stepped over the prostrate form on the stairs he thought her asleep: a homeless person seeking shelter, or a drunk. Reeves saw the pool of blood Crow had missed in the darkness and ran for a policeman, finding PC 226H Thomas Barrett on his beat and bringing him back to see the body.

Unlike Emma, Martha was brutally stabbed to death: there were thirty-nine stab wounds to her body. Most of her organs were pierced many times, but only one blow had pierced her heart, this being given as the cause of death by Dr Timothy Robert Killeen of 68 Brick Lane, who conducted the post mortem examination. Killeen concluded that the wounds were delivered before death, the fatal blow to the heart coming last. There is no record of defensive wounds.

Martha was killed sometime between two o'clock in the morning and half past three. Married couple Joseph and Elizabeth Mahoney had come home at two in the morning, and there had been no-one on the stairs at that point. Exactly what happened remains a mystery.

It is known that Martha was with another prostitute, Mary Ann Connelly (known as 'Pearly Poll') on the evening of 6 August; they picked up a pair of soldiers and went drinking with them along Whitechapel High Street until about a quarter to midnight, when they got down to the serious business of the evening. 'Poll' took her soldier up Angel Alley (which still exists), while Martha took hers up George Yard. Later, at about two in the morning, PC Barrett was patrolling along Wentworth Street when he met a soldier who said he was waiting for his friend, who'd gone off with a girl.

Both Mary Connelly and PC Barrett might be supposed to be able to give evidence of identification, but even though Detective Inspector Edmund Reid arranged identification parades for both to pick out the soldiers concerned, neither managed to do so. The inquest, held in the Working Lad's Institute on Whitechapel Road (which is still standing), was adjourned at the end of the first day to allow DI Reid to continue his investigations, and to identify the body. When the inquest reconvened before Deputy Coroner George Collier, deputising for Coroner Baxter, DI Reid had to admit that no progress had been made, and he finished with a request for information from anyone who might have seen anything.

A Dangerous Area

Both Martha Tabram and, to a lesser extent, Emma Smith have each been claimed as the first Ripper victim, though their deaths did not involve the Ripper signature method of a cut throat followed by mutilation of the dead body and removal of the uterus. However, whether or not they are 'authentic' Ripper victims, their deaths embody the culture of violence in Whitechapel and Spitalfields in the late nineteenth century. Indeed, the term 'Whitechapel' seems to have become linked with violence, as is seen in the case of an attempted murder in October 1888 south of the Thames, in Peckham.[6]

Sarah Brett, living with one Thomas Onley, allows Frank Hall, a messmate of her sailor son, to stay with them. When the 66-year-old Thomas goes out drinking with Hall and both return drunk, he has a huge row with Sarah. Taking his part, Hall slaps Sarah, so she slaps him back, knocking him into a chair. Thomas goes to bed; cursing and as he goes, he tells Hall he'll give him 10s to 'do a Whitechapel murder' on Sarah.

Hall promptly knocks her down and grabs her by the throat; the last thing she remembers is the knife cutting her throat. Fortunately, thanks to her little son calling for the neighbours and the arrival of her sailor son, she survives. Since the wound in itself was not dangerous, and the affray was clearly the result of drunkenness on the part of Onley and Hall, the young man is found guilty of unlawful wounding and sentenced to six months' hard labour.

Both Emma Smith and Martha Tabram lodged on George Street, which no longer exists but was part of a small and sinister area bounded by Commercial Street to the west, Brick Lane to the east, Fashion Street to the north and Wentworth Street to the south. All that survives today is a fragment of the eastern end of Thrawl Street, with the former *Frying Pan* public house on the corner of Thrawl Street and Brick Lane. William Fishman quotes a police spokesman describing George Street in the *East London Advertiser* of 18 August 1888 as 'one of the most dangerous streets in the locality'.[7]

Getting enmeshed with the prostitutes of the George Street area was certainly dangerous, as the sailor Frederick Thomas discovered when, on 19 July 1850, he was lured to George Street by the 18-year-old Eliza Wilson, who picked him up on Ratcliff Highway between midnight and one o'clock. The journey along Dock Street, Leman Street and then most of Commercial Street presumably entailed stops at pubs, because the walk took them about an hour.[8]

Eventually they arrived at 2 George Street and Eliza took him to bed. He was fully clothed, presumably to prevent his clothes being stolen, but this was to prove a vain precaution. After a while, the 23-year-old Sarah Clements came into the room and lay down on top of the bed.

Sometime later, at around a quarter past three, another girl came in, accompanied by three men. All three women then secured Thomas by the head with his sheet and held him while the men stripped him.

Thomas lay alone in the bed after this attack until between eight and nine in the morning, after which he was told to leave. At this point, he was wearing only a shirt and some long canvas underwear. Soon he found a policeman, and the six were rounded up, but most of his property was never recovered; the only thing he saw again was his braces. The defence put up by most of the accused was that Thomas offered his trousers to Eliza Wilson to pay for a bed for the night as he had no money; it did not stand up in court, and all six were sentenced to seven years' transportation.

It was not only those inveigled by the area's prostitutes who became targets for assault, however. Even passers-by could be subjected to violent robberies, as is seen in tales such as that of the robbery of solicitor's clerk Frederick Hardy Jewitt some six months before the assault on Frederick Thomas.[9]

Frederick Jewitt

Somewhere between nine and ten o'clock in the evening of Thursday 10 January 1850, Jewitt is in Whitechapel. He is clerk to his father, a solicitor whose practice is in Lime Street. Jewitt is just recovering from a serious bout of jaundice, and only that morning he was examined by his doctor. What he is doing in Whitechapel is not explained, but he is perfectly sober, having had only a little claret on doctor's orders.

Suddenly he feels someone at his left side: from a quick glance he gets the idea that it is a woman, but that is all. The next thing he knows, a cloth of some kind is pressed over his face, and he loses consciousness.

Between three and four in the morning, William Saunders, a painter who lives in the back room on the top floor at 8 Thrawl Street, hears a noise coming from the room below. Two or three times the noise intrudes into his sleep: it is a faint groan, as if someone were having a nightmare. But he is tired, and goes off to sleep again.

In the morning, Jewitt wakes up in a strange room. Naked but for his socks, covered only by a dirty scrap of a bed sheet, he is lying on what he describes as 'a horrible bed'. He has no idea where he is; he is confused, and in great pain all over. In what morning light penetrates into the room, he makes out that his boots are missing, as are his hat, cashmere shawl, gloves and handkerchief. His waistcoat has been emptied, but has not been taken. His trousers, which were clean the previous evening, are muddy up to the knees, suggesting he has been dragged along in the mud. A quick search reveals he is missing his silver watch, a hair-guard, a tooth-pick and a gold ring, along with change amounting to two shillings and some coppers.

When he tries to open the door, he finds it fastened from the outside. Rattling the door he calls out for help, but then sees a small key on the floor. By now it is between ten and eleven in the morning and John Doward, pot-man at the *Frying Pan* pub on the corner with Brick Lane, has been sent to 8 Thrawl Street to collect pots. Jewitt hears his footsteps in the passage outside; he rattles the door handle again, then he pushes the key under the door. Doward undoes the padlock securing the door and opens up to see Jewitt there in a sorry state, gabbling out his story.

Eventually, the young clerk gets his bearings and goes in search of assistance. Upstairs he finds the painter, Saunders, whom he asks to fetch help from his father's office in the City; Saunders brings back one of the clerks in a cab. As Jewitt is helped into it, he notices that the house is about two hundred yards from where he remembers being attacked.

The thieves behind this attack are Margaret Higgins and Elizabeth 'Fat Bet' Smith. As the cab leaves for the City, Ann Hurley, landlady of 8 Thrawl Street, is in her husband's beer shop at 18 Thrawl Street. She sees Higgins come in, a little the worse for drink, and go over to a man called Gallagher. Higgins buys beer for him and herself and, as they drink, Ann Hurley hears her tell Gallagher that she has fenced some of the goods already. Ann also hears Gallagher say something about 'lag': to be lagged is to be transported.

Ann's child starts crying and she has to go see to it, but she comes back as soon as she can, and will testify later to overhearing Higgins admit to selling the watch, the ring and the scarf, and that she has given Fat Bet her share of the proceeds.

It does not take long for Higgins and Smith to be taken. At about half past ten the following night, Saturday 12 January, Sergeant Thomas Kelly (H2) arrests Higgins in Keate Street, which at that time adjoins George Street. She protests, putting the blame on Fat Bet who, she says, brought Jewitt to the room, robbed him, then 'cut with and stuck to the regulars': in other words, she ran off with the cash and refused to part with any of it. Perhaps realising that there is no point pleading innocence, Higgins protests instead that Fat Bet Smith is just as guilty as she is. She tells Kelly that Smith can be taken in George Street, asking only that Kelly does not reveal that she told him where Fat Bet would be.

It is not until about half past midnight that PC John Johns and another officer take Smith at a house in George Street. Johns goes to the back door, while his colleague knocks on the front door. Immediately Johns hears what he thinks to be a male voice saying, 'So help me God, Bill, it is the copper; hook it!' The back door opens and out bustles Smith, partly undressed. Johns recognises her and after blocking her way, arrests her for the attack. She replies, 'You are mistaken; it was not me, it was the other'. He asks her, 'What other?' She makes no answer.

The attack on Frederick Jewitt was aggravated by his physical infirmity. When attacked by Higgins and Smith, he was getting over a prolonged attack of jaundice, which in adults can cause effects such as abdominal pain and flu-like symptoms. His doctor, Christopher Lerick, describes it in court as 'one of the most serious attacks of jaundice I ever saw in a young person'. The symptoms exhibited by Jewitt suggested that after using chloroform the women had given him laudanum, a tincture of opium and a strong soporific.

The administration of an opiate is confirmed by Jewitt's having vomited copiously. Lerick confirms that an opiate would cause 'copious vomiting' some hours afterwards. A pot boy called David Evans visited the room around midday on the day Jewitt was released and found 'a lot of spew and vomit there', as well as Jewitt's hat and boots under the bed. He graphically describes lifting the bed sheet out of the mess and opening a window. Ann Hurley, the landlady, also describes finding vomit around the room and a chamber pot 'nearly full of vomit'.

This is a serious assault. Jewitt's medical condition, coupled with the use of laudanum on top of chloroform, caused a systematic debilitation which lasted for many days. And so, despite both of them asserting that the key to the room was kept in the lock, that many girls used the house, and that they had never seen Jewitt before, Higgins and Smith, at 23 and 22 years old respectively, are transported to the penal colonies in Australia for fifteen years each.

Jeremiah O'Keefe

The danger lurking in the area did not threaten only the stranger. Some years later, at around half past eight on 31 December 1854, a 48-year-old cooper called Jeremiah O'Keefe decides to celebrate New Year's Eve, not with his wife, but with a prostitute living in Keate's Court, about five minutes' walk from where he lives in Shorter's Rents, Glasshouse Street. She is no stranger; he knows her from Limerick, and has known her for the last five years. Having spent ten minutes with her upstairs in her room, he goes down to wait for her by the door; being suspicious of the occupants of the house, he has his hand over the chain of his silver watch to prevent its being stolen as he descends.[10]

As he is waiting outside, however, he is attacked by three men: a 'garrotting' characteristic of Victorian London's streets.[11] O'Keefe is grabbed by the throat and pulled to the ground, and the gang steal his watch. But these are not unknown assailants. O'Keefe has known James Bedborough for ten or eleven months; he has known Benjamin Rogers for the last two years, and William Merritt for about three. This means that when O'Keefe reports the attack and theft at Leman Street Police Station, he can give a good description of his assailants. In fact, he returns to the station at around a quarter past one in the morning and identifies Rogers and Merritt, who are standing among a small group of men. O'Keefe even goes with the arresting officer, PC H76 George Covill, to arrest Bedborough, who is in bed at 1 Keate Street, a lodging house not far from his father's shop down the road.

Curious as this robbery by known assailants may seem, a more curious development is to come as the trial approaches. The case comes before the Old Bailey Sessions on 29 January 1855, but the night before, there is a last-ditch attempt by the womenfolk of the prisoners to prevent the trial. O'Keefe is drinking in the *Sidney Smith* pub (presumably the one still standing in Dock Street, Shadwell), when he is summoned home. Three women have come to his home; two of them are the mothers of Rogers and Merritt. They have come to offer O'Keefe £2 10s to sign a statement that he will not proceed with the prosecution.

Despite his wife's keenness to take the offer, O'Keefe refuses. Money cannot compensate him for what has been done to him. Besides, the watch and chain cost him nine guineas. He maintains that not even £10 would satisfy him. The women do not give up however; on the morning of the hearing one of them meets him as he is leaving home at nine o'clock. She says, 'Mr Keefe, we have done the best we could, and we could not make up but £2 6s'. He shakes his head and walks away.

All three men are found guilty. Bedborough and Merritt, both aged 20, are sentenced to twelve months' imprisonment. However, the 23-year-old Rogers has already served four months for larceny after being convicted at the Middlesex Sessions the previous May. Accordingly, he is sentenced to four years.

Street Robbery
The small collection of streets around George Street may have been dangerous territory, but the experience of Frederick Jewitt illustrates how predatory local thieves were in the wider vicinity. Even out on the main Whitechapel Road, victims were vulnerable to attack. For instance, on 4 May 1885, John Gwinnel was walking home along Whitechapel High Street when he was accosted by Edward Sear. Despite Gwinnel's denials, Sear insisted that they were old friends and

kept hold of Gwinnel's arm until they reached a side street. Claiming to live along there, Sear tried to pull Gwinnel down the dim alleyway, but he resisted and they tussled until three others joined Sear. Gwinnel was knocked down onto the muddy cobbles and robbed of his watch.[12]

After such assaults the victim was often ready to give chase, despite being outnumbered, the objective being to keep at least one of the gang in sight until the chase alerted a beat policeman. So dogged was Gwinnel in pursuit that twice he managed to get close to Sear who, on both occasions, knocked him down. Still the chase continued until PC H37 Albert Collins came on the scene, catching Sear and taking him into custody. Faced with the mud-spattered victim, Sear resorted to stout denial: PC Collins recalls him saying, 'You are a bloody liar'. After being found guilty, Sear admits to a previous conviction for theft at Chelmsford and is awarded twelve months' hard labour.

When the labourer Edward Mitchell was robbed on Saturday 14 August 1869, the thieves did not even bother with dragging their victim down a side street.[13] Mitchell, of 10 Leigh Street, Stratford, left home at six o'clock in the evening and travelled down to Shadwell to get his pay. With £1 2s 6d in his pocket, he had a drink with his colleagues and then, at about midnight, he headed up to Whitechapel Road to get the bus back to Stratford.

While waiting for his bus, he was approached by the 18-year-old William Carthy, who asked him for some tobacco. Just as Mitchell was fishing it out, Carthy knocked him to the ground. Two other men appeared: one of them, a 16-year-old called William Jones, held Mitchell while the others searched his pockets and took his money. Fortunately for Mitchell, two plain-clothes policemen were nearby and they caught Carthy and Jones as they ran up Osborn Street.

Later that year, between midnight and one o'clock on the morning of 31 October, three men attacked another labourer, William Weller of 77 Minories, as he walked along Whitechapel Road. As with Mitchell, one held Weller while the other two went through his pockets and took 21s and his front-door key. Weller gave chase as they ran off. They passed PC H60 Alfred Woodcock, who seized the 17-year-old John Cole. Another officer, PC H167 Henry Burrows arrived just as

Woodcock was taking his prisoner away and saw Cole drop something, which turned out to be Weller's key.

The attacks on Edward Mitchell and William Weller took place where Whitechapel Road is joined by Osborn Street. All three thieves apprehended were in their teens. Despite their youth, Carthy and Cole were repeat offenders; Carthy received seven years' imprisonment, while his accomplice Jones got only twelve months. Likewise Cole, convicted the previous year under the name of William King, received two years in prison.

It was not only male victims who were prepared to pursue their attackers. On the afternoon of 27 September 1870, for instance, Sarah Klein was walking along Commercial Road with her 80-year-old mother. Just as they had crossed Mulberry Street, a man came up to them; he snatched Sarah's watch (breaking the chain), and her bonnet. Pushing her over on top of her elderly mother, he fled northwards along Mulberry Street followed by an accomplice. He was pursued by Klein, crying, 'Stop thief!' Charles Monk, a clerk, who saw everything, also gave chase, after ensuring the old lady was alright. Meanwhile, Klein had reached Charles Street where she was misdirected by one of the gang to run up New Street, which took her via Fieldgate Street to Whitechapel Road. Though the pursuit was thwarted, the suspects were taken later in a pub on Mile End Road after statements given to the police identified them.[14]

Mrs Esther Samuel, wife of a West Bromwich tailor and draper, was prevented from chasing the three men who beset her in broad daylight on Whitechapel High Street on 27 August 1856, robbing her of a gold chain to which were attached various items including a locket containing a miniature of her husband. The assault took place in the afternoon, as did the assault on Sarah Klein, and in front of what Mrs Samuel described later as 'a great crowd'.[15]

Though Mrs Samuel fought to snatch back her chain, a man identified later as Patrick Bryan, managed to pull it free. The gang ran off up George Yard, heading for the nexus of small streets around George Street. As calling for the police failed to bring assistance (the beat constable, PC H181 John Bone was on his way to Leman Street with another prisoner at the time), Mrs Samuel made to chase the gang herself, but was restrained by the crowd just as she was entering George Yard.

A man in the crowd gave chase, but without success. However, Mrs Samuel's description was such that the 21-year-old Patrick Bryan was caught without difficulty. PC Bone, to whom Bryan was a familiar sight lounging around George Yard, took him the following morning at around eleven o'clock. Bryan's identity was confirmed by a boy, one William Bates, who was on his way to school when the assault happened. He told no-one about it until he got home and told his mother, who then told a policeman.

A more successful pursuit was carried out by one Ellen Marshall after being robbed by Daniel Duggan. On the evening of 12 March 1870, despite being half throttled by Duggan as he broke her watch away from its chain, Mrs Marshall chased her assailant and his equally strong accomplice as they fled south of Whitechapel High Street down Half Moon Passage. In fact she caught hold of Duggan, and as PC H176 Joseph Marriott came towards them from Great Alie Street, he saw her grappling with him.[16]

Duggan managed to break free and escaped along Duncan Street and Leman Street, heading back up on to Whitechapel High Street, where he collided with PC Samuel Richardson (H48), who confirmed the power of the fleeing Duggan: 'He came at me like a little horse, as hard as he could'. Though knocked to the ground, Richardson managed to get up again quickly enough to grab Duggan and hold him.

The 20-year-old Duggan was a repeat offender and, on his conviction in April 1870, he received seven years' imprisonment.

Attacks on the Police
The climate of violence in the Whitechapel and Spitalfields area was not confined to street robberies, which were, in a way, the successors to the highway robberies carried out in the busy streets of Shadwell a century earlier. This link has been made by William Fishman, who states that '[t]he age-old practice of purse-snatching was being

challenged by 'shootflying', i.e. watch-chain snatching'.[17] There was a general context of violence to which even the police were not immune.

Fishman points out that '[t]he dread of every young and well-informed constable was to be posted to East London's 'H' Division', which included Whitechapel and Spitalfields.[18] As is often the case today, the police were vulnerable even when trying to keep the peace, such as when on Thursday 26 November 1874, PC H225 John Stewart tried to hush a rowdy couple, to prevent them causing a disturbance in the small hours.

At half past one in the morning, PC Stewart was on Boyd Street, between Commercial Road and Cable Street, when a man and a woman came along shouting, the man clearly the worse for drink. As he reported later, Stewart 'requested him to be quiet as the people who had gone to bed wanted to sleep and not to be disturbed at that hour of the morning'. The man, James Price, was in no mood to be told what to do, particularly when, as it transpires, he was in front of his own home. Deciding to resist the constable, Price punched Stewart on the chest; Stewart's helmet flew through the open doorway.[19]

Stewart went inside to retrieve his helmet, but as he bent down he heard Price call, 'Give me a poker, I will have the b[lood]y b[ugge]r out of this; it is my house'. This was followed by a blow on the left side of Stewart's head followed by a hefty blow to the right; dodging the blows, Stewart went further into the house and collided with a table full of crockery. At this point PC H162 William White arrived. His head bleeding, Stewart called to White to secure Price, from whom he had just confiscated a file.

Later that day, Stewart was seen by George Phillips, a surgeon of 2 Spital Square, who saw that the wound on the right side of Stewart's head was a serious one, about four inches long and exposing the pericranium. Known otherwise as the periosteum, this is a membrane below the skin which covers the bones, and is very sensitive. Indeed, Phillips could see some bone had been exposed.

It took eighteen days for the case to come to court, during which time Phillips continued to see Stewart; in court he stated he did not know when Stewart would be able to return to work. Price tried to advance the defence that Stewart hurt his head when he rushed into the house and upset the table full of crockery, but he was found guilty; having two felony convictions already, he received a sentence of five years.

This is a relatively small-scale case, but the violence could quickly escalate, as it had some twenty-two years earlier off of the Whitechapel Road.

Overnight, between Monday 23 and Tuesday 24 February 1852, Police Sergeant Thomas Weakford (H5) is on patrol with two constables, John Harris Bickhill (H149) and Francis Williams (H113). At about two o'clock in the morning they are in Fieldgate Street, just off Whitechapel Road and not far from St Mary Matfelon church. Weakford hears a commotion and goes to the corner of New Street to investigate. There is a crowd of eight or ten persons making a disturbance. Asking them to go home has no effect; the crowd continue making a noise and then start throwing stones and pieces of brick.[20]

Weakford, Bickhill and Williams approach along New Street despite the flying objects, and the group moves off into nearby New Court, still pelting the police with stones. At the mouth of New Court things start to escalate. A chunk of brick hits Weakford on the shoulder and he recognises the man who threw it as John Sullivan. As soon as he makes the arrest, however, the crowd rescues Sullivan and he rushes into 8 New Court, with Weakford in pursuit. It is at 8 New Court that the situation turns very violent indeed.

As Weakford grasps John Sullivan again, Francis Sullivan effects a rescue by striking Weakford down from behind with a piece of wood. As Weakford goes down, a partially-dressed third Sullivan – Honora – knocks off his hat, grabs his hair, and starts scratching viciously at his face and pounding him with her fist. Then a second blow lands on the side of his head, from a piece of iron wielded by either John Sullivan or another of the group, Cornelius Ronan.

Weakford is dazed by this second blow, but not so that he doesn't see his colleague, PC Bickhill, struck on the head by Francis Sullivan who is now wielding a chopper. Francis strikes Bickhill so forcefully that he splits the regulation 'stovepipe' hat, a hat so strong that an officer can stand on it. Another of the group, Mary Donovan, immediately sees her opportunity and whacks Bickhill on the head with part of a trestle, causing him to drop his staff. She is described later as having no clothes on.

As Bickhill struggles to regain his staff from John Sullivan, he sees Francis Sullivan busy again with his chopper, bringing it down heavily on the head of PC Williams. Blood spurts up from the wound and flies into Bickhill's face. Sergeant Weakford also sees this and tries to help, but he is forced back against the stove. Seemingly, Honora Sullivan still has hold of Weakford's hair; he later describes her as being more violent than the men.

But now the mob wants to get rid of the badly beaten officers. Williams is pushed back to the door by Francis Sullivan and Mary Donovan. As they go, Honora Sullivan, who presumably has let go of Weakford's hair, hits Williams in the mouth with a stool. Williams is badly hurt and makes his escape out of the window. Weakford makes his way towards the door but is brought down and then thrown out.

Reinforcements have arrived, however; at least three more officers have come, although only one is named at the trial. PC 66H John Mackay enters the house to see Francis Sullivan standing with the chopper still in his hand. He also sees one Mary Canty; she is handing bricks to Matthew Canty, who is throwing them at the police outside. One of them hits the unnamed PC 217H on the shoulder. Then more weapons appear, in the form of reaping hooks.

Mary Canty, the brick passer, picks up a chamber pot and throws it at Mackay, hitting him on the shoulder. It is not specified whether it is empty or full. As this happens, Mackay sees Francis Sullivan swing the chopper again, and Cornelius Ronan makes a rush at PC 178H with a knife in his hand.

The trial record does not state what happened after this, nor how the riot was quelled, but Weakford describes being helped out of New Court, at which point he passed out. Williams was bleeding heavily from the head. When the case comes to trial on 5 April, well over a month later, the defence witnesses tell of a great police presence invading the house. One John Wood claims to have seen the police bring out John Sullivan and beat him. Next-door neighbour Richard Thomas says that from his window he saw four or five policemen beat one man, and then go in and bring out another man in his shirt.

Of those brought to trial, five plead guilty. Four receive twelve months apiece: John and Francis Sullivan, the most active men in the riot, Cornelius Ronan and Michael Harding. Harding does not come into the witness statements of any of the officers, although his wife Catherine states that after she was awoken by the noise, she 'saw a policeman come and take my husband by the waist and throw him down stairs'.

Matthew Canty pleads guilty, but is recommended to mercy: it is not stated why, nor does any sentence seem to have been passed on him (he is to be called afterwards to receive his sentence, but his name does not recur in the Sessions records). Honora Sullivan, the woman who attacked Sergeant Weakford and hit PC Williams in the mouth with a chair, Mary Donovan, the first to attack PC Bickhill, and Mary Canty, who threw a chamber pot at PC Mackay, are all found guilty and given three months apiece.

Olympus Matthews

Most of the stories of violence occurring in the Whitechapel and Spitalfields area tell of violent robbery or of resistance to the police. There are more unusual stories about violence, however, with a bizarre incidence of violence occurring on the Whitechapel Road in 1862.[21]

On the night of Tuesday 12 August, between 10 and 11 o'clock, an engine driver called Olympus Matthews is walking along the Whitechapel Road. Suddenly he feels the pain of a blow to the left side of his jaw. It is so powerful it knocks him down. While on the pavement trying to gather his senses he feels an agonising blow to his left shoulder. So powerful is the second blow that it deprives him of the use of his left arm. Finally managing to take in what is happening, Matthews notices what he recognises to be a piece of a crutch fall from his injured shoulder. At this point he becomes aware of someone above him and looks up just in time to see a man deliver a hefty blow with the crutch to his right arm. So heavy is the blow that the crutch breaks into three pieces.

By now, Matthews has begun to recover himself and he struggles to his feet. A crowd has been gathering to watch the spectacle, but seemingly, going by his testimony later in court, Matthews gets no help from them: 'I found I could not handle him myself, and I sung out for the police'. However, a 'single woman' (often a euphemism in the Proceedings for a prostitute) called Sarah Crawley, who is among the crowd, apparently also calls out for the police. She has seen Matthews beaten, and can see how badly he is bleeding.

PC Joseph Wilkins (H 213) is on the scene soon and he arrests the assailant, picking up the pieces of crutch from the pavement. Matthews is bleeding heavily, has clearly been seriously injured, and accompanies Wilkins and the mystery assailant to Leman Street. When Granger Tandy, a surgeon of 7 Spital Square, comes to Leman Street to examine Matthews, he finds that though the initial blow did not damage the jaw, Matthews has been 'severely wounded' and has lost a lot of blood. Even when the case comes to court Matthews is still unable to use his left arm as a result of his injured shoulder. This is confirmed by Tandy, who is still treating Matthews.

The assault seems completely unmotivated. The assailant is 28-year-old Joseph Coulson who is crippled, having lost 'the greater part' of his foot. He is totally unknown to Olympus Matthews, who can account for the assault only by assuming that Coulson has mistaken him for another man. Just before he charges Coulson with violent assault and takes him off to Leman Street, PC Wilkins overhears him say to Matthews, 'I suppose you thought a cripple could not fetch you down, but I will let you know all about it when we get to the station'. However he does not; nor does he answer when, on the way to Leman Street, Matthews asks him frequently why he assaulted him.

When, on Monday 18 August, the case comes before the Old Bailey sessions, Coulson's defence, as recorded in the Proceedings, is a curious one. He claims that as he was walking along the road, someone grabbed his crutch and used it to strike Matthews down. This stranger then called a crowd together and asked them to arrest Coulson. Having done so, he ran away, leaving the crutch at Coulson's feet. This is not believed; he is found guilty, and given eighteen months in prison.

This curious case of assault may have been caused by a mental health issue, or maybe Coulson did mistake his victim and decided not to admit to it. Whatever the answer, it is another illustration of a violent attack carried out in front of spectators on Whitechapel Road in broad daylight. The lack of motivation makes the case stand out; the violence on the street does not. As has been seen, bright daylight and the presence of strangers were not necessarily deterrents for the thief. The chance-taking by these thieves, and their relative youth (mostly the thieves are in their teens or early twenties), recall the exploits of violent highway robbery on the streets of Shadwell and Stepney encountered earlier in this study.

Chapter 9

Poison for the Asking

Poisoning is associated readily with Victorian Britain. Adulteration of foodstuffs to increase profit margins brought a rise in accidental poisonings.[1] There are, however, many cases of the misuse of poisons and other toxic substances which go to show how ready-to-hand danger was in the new metropolis. Indeed, as Liza Picard points out in her study *Victorian London*, '[a]n astonishing number of poisons were ready to a murderer's hand in the average home'.[2]

Moreover, free access to poisonous substances meant that it was not difficult to come by the means of killing someone over the counter. Legislation was slow to catch up; it was not until 1851 that the Arsenic Act was introduced to try and prevent accidental poisoning with this tasteless and odourless substance. But it was only when the 1868 Pharmacy Act defined just what a pharmacy was, that the definition of who could, and could not, sell toxic substances, including arsenic, was laid down.

William Hinchcliff
Poisoning cases, through their relatively intimate nature, provide an insight into human interrelations in Victorian society. Most disturbing are the cases where young people have attempted poisoning. In her exploration of the poisoning by arsenic of one George Bodle and his family in 1833, Sandra Hempel describes a satirical cartoon printed in an edition of *Punch* magazine in 1846 showing a little girl buying toxic substances over the counter, entitled *Fatal Facility, or Poisons for the Asking*.[3] The ease with which toxic substances could be obtained by children gave them the facility to realise vengeful thoughts towards those they perceived to have wronged them.

One instance of the use of poison to get revenge occurred at the East London Industrial School.[4] Located at 4 Mansell Street (renumbered in 1869 as 96), Goodman's Fields, the building has long since disappeared. Though its name might suggest that it offered evening classes for social improvement, it was in fact an example of the drive during the nineteenth century to improve the lot of the poorer members of the working class. Such initiatives were widespread in Victorian Britain, but nowhere was their presence as concentrated as in the East End of London.

The East London Industrial School started on 31 July 1854 as the East London Shoeblack Society, one of a number of Shoeblack Brigades created in London in the 1850s to offer homeless and destitute boys not just refuge, but also employment. Boys were taken in (up to eighty could be accommodated at Mansell Street) and given work as shoeblacks, who polished people's shoes on the streets. Nearly five years later, on 1 July 1859, the East London Shoeblack Society expanded to become the East London Industrial School, one of a number of such establishments created for the accommodation of juveniles convicted of lesser crimes. The schools also now took in homeless and vagrant children and those who could not be controlled by their parents.

As well as being given a rudimentary education, industrial school pupils were trained in manufacturing processes, which included how to make bags, brushes, blacking and ink, and in the processes of printing. Given how routine the application of corporal punishment was at the time it was perhaps inevitable that, among a group of young convicts, one or more would kick against the regime and, in January 1873, there was an attempted poisoning.[5]

John Bowden, assistant master in charge of teaching the making of brushes and paper bags, found it necessary to discipline the 11-year-old William Hinchcliff in June 1872 for what he called 'schoolboy tricks'. His method sounds brutal to modern sensibilities, but would no doubt have raised few objections at the time. He admitted in court that he grabbed Hinchcliff's ear and dragged him from his stool. He then 'put him to his work'.

What further discipline was meted out by Bowden after this is not stated in the Proceedings. However, two of Hinchcliff's fellow pupils testified that the attempted poisoning was because Bowden had flogged him; in revenge, Hinchcliff, now 12 years old, began doctoring Bowden's tonic.

According to his own testimony, Bowden had been taking medicine for three months before the incident in question. The expert witness, Dr James Scott Sequira, testified that the tonic seemed to contain quinine, an ingredient which is noted for its analgesic qualities. Perhaps Bowden was having difficulties in coping with his pupils? He must have placed a degree of trust in them, however, because he kept his tonic in the store-room cupboard where the boys kept their slippers. James Gibbons and William Marsden, the two pupils who testified in court, both confirmed that they and Hinchcliff knew where the tonic was kept.

What is curious is that Hinchcliff seems to have been prepared to keep adding substances to the tonic until something took effect.[6] Both Gibbons and Marsden testified that on Tuesday 7 January, Hinchcliff put a liquid into the tonic bottle; Gibbons described it as 'lotion what you bathe your eyes with'. Bowden noticed later that day that his tonic tasted more bitter than usual, but otherwise seems to have experienced no ill effects. Two days later, Hinchcliff added a white powder to the mix in the bottle.

The powder was described by Gibbons and Marsden as 'cypric powder' and 'cypitate powder', presumably their attempts at citric acid powder, as used in making lemonade; Dr Sequira revealed, however, that the powder added was 'ammonia chloride of mercury', otherwise known as aminomercuric chloride. A white crystalline solid, aminomercuric chloride is extremely poisonous when ingested, though Dr Sequira described it to the court as not life-threatening. This might be because mercury was not then understood to be poisonous. However, he does testify that one dose of the tonic laced with the powder would have resulted in a burning in the throat, nausea, and a pain in the bowels which would 'temporarily inconvenience' Bowden.

Thankfully for the assistant master, when he took his dose the morning after the tonic had been poisoned, he experienced merely a dry mouth and a feeling of burning. The bitterness he noticed in the tonic after Hinchcliff spiked it the previous Tuesday presumably made him cautious; peering into the bottle he noticed a white deposit floating in the contents which he described in court as a scum. This prompted him to hand over the bottle to the superintendant of the school, who passed it in turn to Dr Sequira.

Hinchcliff's apparent brazenness, or at least insouciance, is a noteworthy feature of the case. Bowden states that after his enquiries led him to confront the boy, Hinchcliff confessed to having put some white powder in the tonic. Moreover, after apparently persuading a day boy called Loughton to get the powder, Hinchcliff seems to have told him, in the presence of Gibbons and Marsden, that he intended to poison Bowden with it. Loughton told PC Thomas Payne (1HR) that Hinchcliff gave him a penny to buy a powder for poisoning some rats, but that after he handed it over, Hinchcliff told him 'We are going to put it into John's medicine'. There was nothing covert about this incident.

Hinchcliff was found guilty of unlawfully and maliciously administering poison to John Bowden with intent to aggrieve him, and with intent to annoy him. Curiously, he is not found guilty of administering poison to Bowden with intent to injure him. For this, Hinchcliff is sentenced to three years in Feltham Reformatory, the original industrial school. Founded by its own Act of Parliament in 1854 as the Middlesex County Industrial School for Boys, it could accommodate 700 boys aged from 7 to 13. It also got boys out of the urban environment into the countryside to teach them a variety of skills, including cookery and, aboard the training brig *Endeavour*, nautical skills.[7]

Susannah Field

An under-age poisoning case which is perhaps more sinister than the Hinchcliff case is the attempted poisoning by the 15-year-old Susannah of her mother, Mary Ann Field.[8] On 15 January 1891, Mary Ann was sitting by the fire at their home at 8 Mercer Street, Shadwell. The street no longer exists but then, flanked by Twine Court and King David Lane, it connected Cable Street to the Ratcliff Highway. Mary Ann had been ill and taking medicine all through the winter.

Shortly after one in the afternoon she sent her daughter with three halfpence and a clean mug to get some porter from the pub. The nearest pub was the *Crooked Billet* in King David Lane (the street is still there, but the pub is long gone). Susannah could have been there and back within five minutes if she got swift service, but she was gone a long time, and came back with a mug of flat beer, saying that she had been talking with a neighbour who wished her mother better.

Taking a sip of porter, Mary Ann thought it had a nasty taste. While the girl blamed the medication for this, her mother could not bring herself to drink any more, and she emptied it into a bucket which had some dirty water in it. This revealed 'about a small teaspoonful of green grits' in the bottom of the mug. She sent her daughter back to the pub to complain.

In the meantime another girl, Annie Miles, had retrieved from the gutter the small bottle that Susannah had emptied into the beer mug before going home, and taken it to her own mother. Annie's mother, along with her next-door neighbour Mrs Turner, went to Mercer Street to confront Susannah and to ask her what she had done. When the girl denied attempting to murder her mother, Mrs Miles took the bottle to the police.

Shadwell Police Station stood on the corner of King David Lane and Juniper Street; only a short stretch of Juniper Street survives, and the site of the police station is occupied by late twentieth century housing. It was at this station that Mrs Miles spoke to Inspector John Quinn and showed him the bottle, labelled 'T James's Phosphor Paste'. Quinn had the bottle taken to the practice of Dr Robert Heatley at 29 King David Lane for him to examine, and headed for 8 Mercer Street to speak to the Fields. Susannah by this time had gone out, but it wasn't long before he arrested her in Cable Street, to the north of Mercer Street. When he told her why she was being arrested, she burst into tears but said nothing.

Shortly afterwards, in the charge room in the custody of PC James Alder (H377), Susannah made a statement. In it she confessed that she tried to poison her mother at the suggestion of a young woman called Kate Dudley, who lived at 83 Lucas Street (another lost street: nearby, but on the north side of Cable Street). Susannah claimed that Dudley had promised her that, after she was married, she would look after Susannah. Her statement blamed Dudley's prompting for her buying a pennyworth of phosphorus paste from Emily Watley's oil and colour shop at 336 Cable Street. She claimed that Dudley had been with her when she bought it, and also when she asked little Annie Miles to hold the mug of beer while she emptied the paste into it. She claimed also that Dudley had told her what to say should anything come to light.

Kate Dudley denied any involvement in the attempted murder; she said that she knew Susannah Field only by sight, and had seen Mary Ann Field only twice: at the Magistrate's Court, and now at the Old Bailey. That she does not seem to have been charged with complicity in the murder suggests that she was believed.

The attempted poisoning was a clumsy one. The poison selected was not soluble, and thus most of it sank to the bottom of the beer. The penny that Susannah used to buy it was not her own money, but a penny she borrowed from their neighbour Alice Roffey, who lived at 16 Mercer Street. She borrowed it on her way to buy the beer. Moreover, the fact that she asked Annie Miles to hold the mug while she emptied the bottle into it using a hairpin, and then threw the bottle into the gutter, providing an opportunity for Annie to retrieve it, shows that Susannah had no idea what to do.

Maybe it was all based on a fantasy concocted by a girl desperate to leave home but with no hope of doing so? Perhaps she projected her fantasy on an innocent neighbour, who may have made an ambivalent remark which caused Susannah to concoct a fantasy in which the young woman would take Susannah away from the confines of life with her mother and into her new home, where they would work together. Susannah's father was a ship's cook and was thus liable to be away from home for long periods of time. When the case came to trial on 9 February 1891, he was away at sea, and had been for a year.

The last we hear of Susannah Field is her plea in defence that 'I wish the young woman would own to it; she knows it is the truth'. She was then sentenced to three months' hard labour. What her home life was after she served her sentence is of course lost in the mists of time. That is on the assumption that Susannah had a home waiting for her when she came out.

Martha Sharp
Not all poisoning was malicious. Sometimes dangerous substances could be applied as a result of an ignorance of the effects they produced. This would not always cause the death of the victim; sometimes it would result in a violent but temporary and curable physical disorder, as in July 1850, when unreciprocated passion nearly killed someone who had no connection whatever with the poisoned desires of Martha Sharp.[9]

On 23 July 1850, while in mid-performance on stage at the Pavilion Theatre, Whitechapel, James Walker Elphinstone spots an extremely unwelcome audience member: a woman called Martha Sharp, sitting in a box and watching him keenly. For four months Sharp has been haunting the happily married Elphinstone, accompanied by a friend called Mrs Holborough who has been acting as her go-between. Not daring to approach Elphinstone herself, she has always held back, sending over Mrs Holborough to ask him to come and walk with Miss Sharp, and to have a little conversation with her; invariably he has declined the invitation.

Eventually, Martha Sharp escalated the process by sending Elphinstone a note, again via Mrs Holborough, which he burned. He saw the two women later that evening, but turned and walked away without speaking.

The following evening, Elphinstone stopped off 'at the public house at the corner' for a beer on his way home. Presumably this was the former *Black Bull*, now a restaurant, standing on the corner of Whitechapel Road and Vallance Road. When he got to the bar, however, he saw Miss Sharp and Mrs Holborough standing there. In a nightmare moment, Mrs Holborough came over and asked him to take some gin and water; he declined, presumably none too graciously. Having stepped up her campaign, however, Sharp seems to have resolved to take more decisive action to snare the affections of the obstinate performer.

Seemingly, Martha Sharp is not accompanied in the box at the Pavilion by Mrs Holborough on 23 July; at some point she leaves the box and heads to the stage door, where she stands, waiting for someone to help her. Presently she sees William Davis, a waiter from the *King's Head* pub further up Baker's Row (now Vallance Road: the pub was demolished sometime after 1921). She stops him, gives him a paper bag, and asks him to take it in to Elphinstone for her. Being a waiter, presumably Davis is used to being sent on errands; without opening the bag, he takes it in and hands it over to Elphinstone's dresser, Thomas King. Davis does not say who sent it. King opens up the bag and looks inside: it contains a twopenny jam tart with a latticed pastry top.

However tempting the tart, Elphinstone refuses it. Maybe he can guess who sent it. He tells King he can do what he likes with it, so the dresser decides to take it home and give it to his wife Charlotte. That evening she eats a little of the crust, but then lays it aside; it is not until the following morning that she demolishes most of the tart. By the time Thomas gets up there is only a little left, a round piece at the centre, and Charlotte King is being violently sick. She brings up the undigested tart; alarmingly there is blood in the vomit. She remains in considerable pain for the rest of the day; she is still under the doctor when the case comes to court on 19 August.

Seemingly, King leaves his wife suffering at home and goes to work; maybe she persuaded him that he had to keep his employer sweet. Whatever the reason, it is Elphinstone who calls in Dr Henry Thomas Cornelius of 71 Whitechapel High Street. Cornelius examines the tart and sees all too clearly what has happened. Mrs King left the middle of the tart because under the jam she saw 'green stuff'. Cornelius identifies the green stuff as cantharides: Spanish fly.

(The Spanish fly is actually a green beetle, one of the 'blister beetles', so called because they secrete cantharidin, a defensive secretion which causes blisters. Because of its irritation of the genitals and the consequent increased blood flow, it has been considered for centuries to be an aphrodisiac.)

Not only was Martha Sharp mistaken in her hopes that the Spanish fly would act on Elphinstone to stimulate his desire, she was also unaware of how to prepare it. Cornelius states in court that when employed as an aphrodisiac, Spanish fly is used as a tincture. Martha Sharp, however, used partially ground beetles: 'bruised, not powdered' according to the doctor. He finds 'a considerable quantity of cantharides' in the tart, 'portions of several flies' in fact, and though unfamiliar at first hand with the effects of ground beetles, he estimates that the concentration could well have proved fatal.

Depending on how much is taken, cantharidin can strip away the stomach lining completely.[10] However, though she suffers terribly from the after-effects of ingesting some of the beetle parts, Mrs King survives. Later, on trial at the Old Bailey Sessions for attempted murder, Martha Sharp is found not guilty. It is decided that she had no way of knowing that the tart would be eaten by Mrs King, and the judge Sir Thomas Platt asks the jury whether as regards Elphinstone 'the other intention suggested', i.e. using Spanish fly as an aphrodisiac, might not be the more probable explanation of Martha's actions than that she sought to kill him. Clearly they agree. This is a grim episode, but at least no-one dies. The same cannot be said of the case of Henry Steward Davis.

Henry Davis

Henry Davis was a youth who, like the neglected Joseph Lipman who died in Boar's Head Yard, had serious care needs. During the manslaughter trial which followed his death in 1851, he is described as being 'very imbecile indeed', seemingly 'quite idiotic', and it is said that 'his faculties were very much impaired'. Unlike Joseph Lipman, however, Henry Davis was killed with kindness.

Henry's condition would seem to have been a congenital one. His mother, not named in the trial record, had lodged for four months with William and Elizabeth Wanstall of 85 Ratcliff Highway when, according to Mrs Wanstall, she left Henry with them 'to go into the country'. On her return, she was removed to the workhouse on grounds of being insane. Five weeks later, Henry was dead.[11]

After Henry's mother has been confined in the workhouse, Elizabeth Wanstall takes it upon herself to look after him. She has three children, and she cares for him as if he were one of her own, but she is not up to the task of giving the care he requires. He has a history of internal disorder, which has manifested itself as abdominal discomfort and pain, and in bouts of constipation. His mother would treat them by dosing him frequently with rhubarb and by giving him enemas. Latterly, however, she was giving Henry composition powder, a herbal treatment containing a mixture of ingredients and used as a cure-all.

It is not surprising that, while living with the Wanstall family, Henry's mother should have begun using a popular herbal remedy to settle her son's long-term bowel complaint. Mr Wanstall is in the employ of John Stephens, a medical botanist with a considerable local business, whom Mrs Wanstall describes as an 'agent of Dr Coffin' (Albert Isaiah Coffin, an American herbalist who in 1838 brought a new style of herbal medicine from the United States to England).

Mr Stephens seems to be the medical authority for the Wanstall family. Elizabeth Wanstall says that she has known him for more than twelve months, and that he medicates her and her children. She testifies in court to how careful and attentive he is, and that she did not ask any of the local doctors to attend Henry. She seems not to be unusual in this. William Crocker, his shopkeeper, testifies that Stephens makes house calls to those who buy his preparations 'if they want him', and that people have sent for him as a medical man.

It is John Stephens who is accused of causing Henry's death through medicating him and, though Stephens is found not guilty, the case shows how dangerous ignorance about the active ingredients in generally accepted preparations can be. As with the overdose of Spanish fly prepared by Martha Sharp, the herbal medication given to Henry Davis was not meant to harm him; sadly those who administered it didn't understand that it was dangerous for someone in Henry's condition.

Henry's ordeal begins on Thursday 10 July, when his bowels give him trouble, worsening on the following day. The Wanstalls treat him with a little gruel and with warm flannels on the stomach. However, the complaint persists over the weekend and on Monday she is roused to action; not to seek out a doctor, but to go to Mr Stephens.

Stephens tells her, 'Go and get a little composition powder'. He does not specify how much should be given, so she gives Henry a half teaspoonful mixed in some raspberry tea. He does not take it however, and instead it goes all over his face, clothes and bedding. She does not say how it spreads so far: whether Henry knocks it away, or whether she tries to administer it by force.

On Tuesday she gives him rhubarb and places a mustard plaster on his stomach, but this does no good so, on Wednesday, she returns to Stephens. As well as instructing her to give more composition powder, Stephens decides it is time to administer an enema, which he does at around eight that evening, helped by Mr Wanstall and using the syringe Henry's mother used when giving Henry his enemas. The enema is made up of composition powder with preparations of lobelia and of valerian added.

At first it seems to be the answer, and Henry spends a peaceful night and seems better on the next morning, but this does not last and he sinks rapidly in the afternoon. At last Mrs Wanstall is stirred to seek a doctor, but the doctor she calls on is not in. Meanwhile, Mr Wanstall is also looking for a doctor, and he manages to bump into Dr Mark Garrett on the street; he comes to see Henry, but it is too late.

When the case comes to court, the principle issue to be resolved is the effect of composition powder. It is consumed often by the Wanstall household; Elizabeth Wanstall testifies that it 'never made me ill; it has always done me a great deal of good, and my children too'. Moreover William Crocker, the shopkeeper, testifies that he has taken 'pounds' of it, and he praises it: 'It has made me a great deal better than I used to be. It has done me good'. He points out also that the shop sells 'a great deal of it'.

It may be beneficial in a general way, but for Henry Davis it was to prove fatal, the reason being the inflamed condition of his bowels. Thomas Overton, Constable of the Parish, buys some composition powder from Stephens' shop to give to Dr Henry Letheby, a lecturer at London Hospital and specialist in the subject of poisons and their effects on the human frame who is interested in the case. As Overton buys the powder he sees Stephens, who explains that the powder contains bayberry bark, hemlock bark, ground ginger, cloves and cinnamon. Stephens says that the bayberry bark, hemlock bark and ground ginger are astringent. After a moment he also admits that there was lobelia in the enema administered to Henry. Later when he analyses the sample, Letheby detects cayenne pepper also.

The composition powder administered to Henry Davis therefore contained various ingredients the purpose of which was to irritate, and thus stimulate, the intestines, drawing more blood into them and making them more active. This would be the case when the powder is taken orally; but it was administered to Henry also as an enema, with the addition of lobelia, which also works as an irritant. After post mortem examination, both Dr Garrett and Dr Letheby stress the inflamed nature of Henry's digestive tract.

Garrett and Letheby ascribe Henry's death to inflammation of the intestines. Letheby describes his lower intestines as being so inflamed 'that they were nearly disorganised, nearly in a pulpy state, in the highest state of inflammation'. His opinion is that the enema administered by Stephens 'would increase the inflammation, and it would be the very worst thing that could possibly be applied'.

Garrett is concerned about composition powder. Having had no experience of it before, he has been investigating it and experimenting, recreating the enema of composition powder, lobelia and valerian. Given the amount of stimulation caused to the bowels of dogs when lobelia, valerian and composition powder were given orally, he considers the compound to be dangerous.

Interestingly, there seem to be indicators in his statements that Garrett is being accused of partiality. His statement that 'I know of no quarrel between myself and the prisoner' is an unconnected one, seemingly in answer to a direct question suggesting animosity between the two men. Certainly Garrett seeks to belittle the popularity of herbal medications. His statement 'I heard of a meeting at which Dr Coffin gave a lecture; I was not present' sounds offhand.

Garrett's statement, 'I do not know that this person's medicines were very generally taken' is belied, however, by Crocker's testimony to the popularity of Stephens locally. Moreover, the enthusiasm for composition powder shown at the trial by Elizabeth Wanstall and William Crocker would seem to reflect its more general popularity; Crocker states that the shop sells 'a great deal of it'.

Though Stephens is found not guilty of causing the death of Henry Davis, the misapplication of such a non-specific cure-all remedy shows how dangerous ignorance could be. Indeed, Liza Picard cites *The Magazine of Domestic Economy* to show not just how dangerous medications bought over the counter could be, but also how dependent on such self-medication Victorian Britain became.[12] Death and peril lurk in the new urban setting of the Victorian metropolis, where children can gain access to toxic substances over the counter and people administer compounds in ignorance of how much damage can be done by their misuse. The conditions of the poor East End seem to encourage this danger, as people are squashed up against each other, poverty is rife, and a sense of perspective is lost in the new urban society.

Israel Lipski
The above cases of poisoning and near poisoning reveal much about social conditions in metropolitan London. There is, however, a case of deliberate poisoning which, in his study *The Trials of Israel Lipski,* Martin Friedland claims to be embroiled in one of the major social issues of London in the 1880s, the reception of an influx of Ashkenazi Jewish refugees fleeing persecution in German and Russian controlled territories.

In its time, the case featured heavily in the press and caused huge public interest. Israel Lipski, a Polish Jew who made walking sticks at 16 Batty Street, south of Commercial Road[13] and who therefore used nitric acid professionally, was arrested and tried for the murder of Mrs Miriam Angel by pouring acid into her mouth while she lay unconscious in her bed.[14]

On the morning of 28 June 1887, Dinah Angel is beginning to worry. Usually her daughter-in-law Miriam arrives between half past eight and nine o'clock for breakfast, but she has not turned up. Mrs Angel decides to go round to the house on Batty Street where Miriam lives and see whether she is alright. Batty Street is just to the east of Berner Street (now Henriques Street) where, just over a year later, the body will be found of Elizabeth Stride, the third victim of Jack the Ripper.

Mrs Angel arrives at 16 Batty Street around eleven o'clock. Just as she arrives, two women of the house are returning from shopping on Petticoat Lane. One is Leah Lipski, wife of Philip Lipski, tailor; she and her husband live with their seven children in the two ground-floor rooms, and sub-let the other two floors. The other woman is Leah Levy, the estranged wife of one Abraham Levy; she shares the first-floor back room with Leah Lipksi's mother-in-law, Mrs Rachel Rubenstein. Mrs Rubenstein herself is sitting outside the house on a chair when they return.

Mrs Lipski and Mrs Levy follow Mrs Angel as she heads upstairs to the first floor front room, where Isaac and Miriam Angel live. Isaac, a boot riveter, left for work that morning between a quarter past and half past six. At that time, his wife Miriam was still in bed. It is now after eleven o'clock. There is no answer to Mrs Angel's knock at the door. Mrs Levy peers through the keyhole, but the key is in the lock, so Leah Lipski goes up to the small window at the half-landing. She is joined by Leah Levy and Dinah Angel as she gazes down to see Miriam Angel lying motionless in bed, only half-dressed and with her body largely exposed.

'She looks bad', is Mrs Levy's opinion; 'Perhaps she is fainting?' ventures Mrs Angel. The three women then rush down to the bedroom door and break it open. Miriam Angel does not stir, and Leah Lipski takes a close look at her: she is dead, and there are acid burns on her face and chest.

Mrs Lipski runs noisily to fetch the doctor, and the commotion calls down the men working upstairs on the second floor, Simon Rosenbloom and Richard Pitman. They work for Israel Lipski (no relation to Philip and Leah Lipski), who rents the single second-floor room where he makes walking sticks. Lipski himself has not been seen since ten o'clock, when he came in and then went out again after about five minutes. Rosenbloom enters the Angels' room just in time to see Dinah Angel faint.

After this, people begin to converge on the room. William Piper arrives with Leah Lipski. Piper is the assistant to Dr Kay of 100 Commercial Road, who was out when Mrs Lipski called. He orders that Mrs Angel be removed from the room and kept out. As she is being removed, Harris Dyween arrives. He is a general trader at 52 Fairclough Street, at the other end of Batty Street, and was summoned by the noise. Passing Dinah Angel on the stairs he goes into the room, sees Miriam Angel lying half-clothed in bed, and covers her up, at which point Piper clears the room and locks it.

Soon after this Dr Kay arrives, Mrs Lipski having gone out again and intercepted him in his carriage. He and Piper, accompanied by Dyween and Rosenbloom, go back in to examine the body. There are acid marks on Mrs Angel's mouth, neck and chest; clearly she has swallowed acid and, as the door was locked from the inside, with the key still in the lock, suicide would be a natural assumption. The glass by the bed contains traces of beer but nothing else, so a search ensues to find a bottle. Dyween looks under the bed; moving an egg box containing old clothes, he sees another body.

It is as PC Arthur Sack (H389) comes in that the bed is pulled from the wall, revealing the unconscious Israel Lipski, who has acid burns in his mouth and on his hands. He is not dead and is soon revived, at least in part, by Kay, who questions him without result in English and German. Sack then takes Lipski away as another policeman, PC H431 Alfred Inwood, arrives. Shortly afterwards, Isaac Angel rushes into the house, alerted by Mrs Levy, but he is not allowed to enter the room; he is kept from the room all that day.

Sack steers Lipski through a gathering mob to the police station, where he is seen by the divisional surgeon, and then to London Hospital. Meanwhile, Inspector David Final arrives at Batty Street and examines the lock; he finds all in order, considering it has been forced open. The condition of the lock is crucial to the case, given that the door was found locked from the inside with the key in the lock.

At the hospital Israel Lipski's stomach is pumped and the acid burns on his hands and mouth are examined, as are the scratches and abrasions on his hands and arms. Later, Inspector Final arrives with Henry David Smedge, an interpreter living on Leman Street who has interpreted at the Thames Police Court for years. After he has been cautioned, Lipski makes a statement through Smedge, claiming he was himself a victim of assault at the hands of two men he took on to work for him.

Some days previously, having left the employ of Mark Katz (called 'Mr Macartz' in the Proceedings) of Watney Passage, Commercial Road, to set up as a stick maker in his own right, Lipski took on two former colleagues, Richard Pitman and Simon Rosenbloom. The day before the attack on Miriam Angel, he also engaged a Russian locksmith called Isaac Schmuss, whom he found at the general store run by Mark Schmidt at 94 Backchurch Lane.

On the morning of 28 June, Lipski was in and out, at one point asking Rosenbloom to get some brandy for dissolving shellac to make varnish. As he left for the second time Schmuss arrived, so Lipski sent him up to the workshop. On returning from a visit to the yard, he was going back upstairs when, he claims, he met Rosenbloom and Schmuss in the doorway of the Angels' room on the first floor (the workshop being on the second).

They took hold of him by the throat and threw him to the ground; they opened his mouth and poured in poison saying, 'That is the brandy'. Securing his hands they then demanded his money and, when he said he had none, his gold watch chain, which was in pawn. Finally they put a piece of wood in his mouth and proceeded to choke him, with the words, 'If you don't give it to us you will be as dead as the woman'; they then took him into the Angels' room, put him beneath the bed, where he passed out, and left him for dead.

When the case comes to court on 29 July, Rosenbloom maintains (through an interpreter) that he stayed in the workshop, breakfasting on bread and butter, from his arrival at seven o'clock until he heard the commotion from downstairs at about eleven. During this time he claims Lipski left the workshop twice and did not return after the second time; Schmuss arrived after the second time, stayed for a quarter of an hour or so, speaking little and in Yiddish, and then left. Rosenbloom denies talking to Pitman in English, as he knows no English, and denies telling him that he knew Schmuss. He denies that Lipski sent him for brandy, and denies intercepting Lipski on the landing with Schmuss.

Schmuss claims, also through an interpreter, that after being admitted by Lipski he went upstairs and remained in the workshop some ten or fifteen minutes, speaking a little to Rosenbloom in Yiddish. As Lipski didn't come in, he left and returned to his lodgings at 60 Oxford Street (now Stepney Way). He denies meeting Rosenbloom before, and denies assaulting Lipski on the first floor. He did not go into Mrs Angel's room; in fact, he did not go into any room other than the workshop, nor did he see Lipski again after entering the house.

An important point is that when Rosenbloom and Schmuss were together in the workroom, the only other person present was the 16-year-old Richard Pitman. Knowing no Yiddish, there was no way he could understand what the two men were saying to each other. Moreover, his testimony challenges Rosenbloom's claim that he speaks no English. Pitman claims that he would speak to him in a mixture, 'half his own language and half our language', so that the boy could not always understand him. He also claims that Rosenbloom told him, in English, that he knew Schmuss.

Most telling is that Pitman left to go home for breakfast, about a quarter of a mile away, leaving Schmuss and Rosenbloom alone in the workshop. Schmuss claims to have stayed 'about a minute's time after he left, not more'; Rosenbloom claims that Pitman was still in the room when Schmuss left. Pitman arrived home at a quarter past nine and was at home for some twenty minutes at the most, but then by his own admission he stopped for 'a little game in the street for about a quarter of an hour' before returning to Batty Street almost an hour after leaving.

It is quite possible, therefore, that Rosenbloom and Schmuss could have attacked Miriam Angel, but Pitman then rules out their attacking Lipski with his statement that, about half an hour after he came back from breakfast, Lipski came into the room and that, when Lipski left five minutes afterwards, Rosenbloom and he were working together in the workshop until the commotion started.

Another important point is the Angels' lock. It was a brand new lock fitted recently, but not by a locksmith. Instead Philip Lipski's landlord, Charles Peters, put it on. A tailor by trade, Peters describes himself in court as 'a practical man', and claims that he has been fixing locks and doing other repairs for about twenty years. The new lock did not fit the hole left by the previous one, so Peters had to put in a wedge beneath it to make it fit. There was also a gap above the lock, sufficient, according to Leah Lipski, to allow three fingers to be poked through it, but not enough to lock the door from outside by turning the key inside.

The three women burst in because they thought that the door was locked from the inside, but was it? Possibly they assumed this because the key was on the inside, blocking the keyhole. Leah Lipski says she did not hear Dinah Angel try the door, nor did she try it herself. Dinah Angel says that she tried the door 'and it was closed', but she is not specific about trying the handle. In fact she says she saw Leah Levy try the handle and say, 'The key is inside'.

Even though the door was broken open, after a little adjustment, William Piper is able to lock the bedroom door to keep everyone out until Dr Kay arrives. Moreover, for some two weeks after the murder the room is let out to another tenant, one Mrs Jacobs. It is not until 20 July, nearly a month after the murder, that the lock is actually sawn off, with a piece of the door and doorframe, to be examined and presented in court. Moreover, according to Leah Lipski and Leah Levy, Sergeant George Bitten himself burst open the door a week before.

Given that the condition of the lock when presented for trial was compromised, and that Pitman going for breakfast left Rosenbloom

173

and Schmuss alone together for the best part of an hour, there is the possibility that they might indeed have killed Miriam Angel. While Charles Peters was not a locksmith, Isaac Schmuss was and no doubt could have locked the door from outside, had it indeed been locked. But Rosenbloom could not have been party to an assault on Israel Lipski if Pitman was telling the truth about his not leaving the room after Lipski was last seen there.

After two days in court, the jury take just eight minutes to find Lipksi guilty; he is sentenced to death, and scheduled to hang on Monday 15 August. Lipski's solicitor John Hayward, however, considers that his client has not been given a fair trial; the defence counsel did not put all the points contained in the brief and, when summing up, the judge steered the jury 'more forcefully than even he was accustomed to do'.[15]

Hayward fights for a reprieve of Lipski's death sentence, publishing a six-page pamphlet arguing his innocence. A week's stay of execution is granted, but no further reprieve can be obtained after this, and Israel Lipski is hanged on Monday 22 August. On the day, Lipski confesses in writing that he is indeed guilty of the murder of Miriam Angel. This is taken as a vindication of the way the trial was conducted, which had been called into question on various levels. However, there are clear inconsistencies in his confession, which cause Friedlander to suspect that there was an ulterior motive on Lipski's part.[16]

The Lipski case gives an insight into many aspects of East End life in the late nineteenth century: multiple occupancy, small-scale industry, makeshift repairs by a landlord who will not get them done properly. It also illustrates clearly the uncertain lifestyle experienced by the local Jewish community, augmented as it was by refugees. These refugees are distanced from the local population by cultural and linguistic barriers; most of the witnesses, as well as Lipski himself, needed the service of an interpreter in court. The reaction to the case is also indicative of the prevalence of anti-Jewish feeling in the area.

Friedland argues cogently that, at time of writing his study (1984), this aspect of the case has not received sufficient attention. He argues also that it might explain why Lipski made his eleventh-hour confession. He suggests that Rabbi Simeon Singer, a regular visitor to Lipski as his spiritual counsellor in Newgate Gaol, may have persuaded him to make a confession which was 'the least damaging to the Jewish community' at a time when the arrival of large numbers of Jewish refugees was causing friction.[17]

In this connection, the Lipski case foretells the increase in anti-Semitic feeling just over a year later, when Jack the Ripper was committing atrocious murders in the vicinity – including the murder of Elizabeth Stride at Dutfield's Yard, one street to the west of Batty Street. Significantly, shortly before she was murdered, a witness saw a woman knocked down on Berner Street as another man on the other side of the road called out 'Lipski!'

Seemingly, the Ripper murders have overshadowed the importance of the Lipski case, but at the time it was a high profile case that jeopardised the career of the Home Secretary, Henry Matthews, and strengthened the call for a Court of Appeal which, ironically, was undermined by Lipski's confession. Moreover, the press attention given to the case, particularly by the *Pall Mall Gazette*, raised the question of trial by media. Moreover, a waxwork of Lipski in his Newgate cell was put in the Chamber of Horrors at Madame Tussaud's shortly after the hanging.[18]

More than any other method of causing harm to another, poisoning would seem to give an insight into the heart of Victorian domesticity; at one time deliberate, at another accidental, it reveals how dangerous people could be to one another. Both affectionate ignorance and malicious opportunism could be equally detrimental. When added to the pressures borne of poverty and overcrowding, together with the changing social values of industrial Britain, poisoning gave the domestic situation in the Victorian East End its most extreme expression.

Notes

Introduction – Old Sins Cast Long Shadows

1 Details from 'The Brutality of night-constables and watchmen', an 'uncited source' of 1825 quoted on www.mernick.org.uk/thhol/ brutality.html, and from *The Examiner* (ed. John hunt) 21 November 1825 747.

2 *The Inheritor's Powder* p.88.

3 Ibid p.84.

4 http://pubshistory.com/LondonPubs/BethnalGreen/King Queen.shtml.

5 *Old East Enders* p.5.

Chapter 1 – The Cutters' Riots

1 Peter Linebaugh claims it was the master weavers who wanted this (*The London Hanged* p.280: 'The 'principal inhabitants of Spitalfields' [...]').

2 Captain Thomas Taylor, testifying at the trial of Nathaniel Norris (see below): www.oldbaileyonline.org, trial reference t17691206-23.

3 *The London Hanged* p.281.

4 www.oldbaileyonline.org, trial reference t17691206-23.

5 *Hanoverian London* p.184.

6 Ibid p.185.

7 Ibid p.191-2.

8 Cf Rudé *Hanoverian London* p.197: 'The weavers had a record of militancy second to none'.

9 Cf Linebaugh *The London Hanged* p.271 (p.260 for the variations on the three basic weaves).

10 Ibid p.286.

11 *The London Mob* p.142.

12 Linebaugh puts Doyle there too (cf *The London Hanged* p.279).

13 Linebaugh refers to a 'code of silence', yet admits that Mary Poor was 'waiting for [the cutters] to buy her silence' (*The London Hanged* p.276).

14 www.oldbaileyonline.org, trial reference t17691018-22.

15 Cf. the letter dated 13 November 1769 from Sawbridge and Townsend, addressed to the king and quoted in *The London Magazine* (eds. Kimber and Kimber 1770) p.37.

16 www.oldbaileyonline.org, trial reference t17691206-34.

17 Letter, 'To the Right Honourable Lord Barrington, Secretary at War' 18 December 1769: cf. Hughson *London* pp.592-3.

NOTES

18 Cf. Linebaugh *The London Hanged* p.278.
19 www.oldbaileyonline.org, trial reference t17691206-31.
20 Cf. Linebaugh *The London Hanged* p.278: 'His expenses in the Old Bailey
trial were paid by Lewis Chauvet [...]'.
21 Details taken from the trial of Henry Stroud, Robert Campbell and Anstis
Horsford for the murder of Daniel Clarke.
22 *The London Mob* p.130.
23 Ibid p.132.
24 Both letters are quoted in *The Scots Magazine* 1771 (ed. James Boswell)
p.219.
25 *The London Hanged* p.281.
26 *Hanoverian London* p.201.
27 *The Annual Register*, 1771 (ed. Thomas English) p.194.
28 Cf the 1784 'List of Prices' appended to the *Abstract* of 1789 (ed. James
Farham) pp.9-54.
29 *Observations* p.2.

Chapter 2 – The Gordon Riots
1 *Hanoverian London* p.227.
2 All details are taken from the record of the trial at www.oldbailey online.org,
reference t17800628-22.
3 All details are taken from the record of the trial at www.oldbailey online.org,
reference t17800628-75.
4 All details are taken from the record of the trial at www.oldbailey online.org,
reference t17800628-23.
5 Details of the looting are taken from the trial records at
www.oldbaileyonline.org of Amelia Hall and Jemima Stafford (reference
t17800628-36) and Mary Stratton (reference t17800628-119).
6 *The London Mob* p.138.
7 Cf the records of the trials at www.oldbaileyonline.org, reference t17800628-
89 (Barrett) and t17800628-25 (Growte).
8 All details are taken from the records of the trials of William Macdonald
(reference t17800628-38), of Thomas Downs (reference t17800628-103) and
of Mary Roberts and Charlotte Gardiner (reference t17800628-65) at
www.oldbaileyonline.org.
9 *The London Mob* p.148.
10 Cf the record of the trial at www.oldbaileyonline.org, trial reference
t17800628-64.
11 Cf the record of the trial at www.oldbaileyonline.org, trial reference
t17800628-35.
12 *The London Mob* p.142.

Chapter 3 – Highway Robbery

1 All details are taken from the record of the trial of John Austin at www.oldbaileyonline.org, reference t17831029-4.

2 Cf *Curiosities of London Street Literature* p.173.

3 All details are taken from the record of the trial at www.oldbailey online.org, trial reference t17400903-16.

4 *Hanoverian London* p.96.

5 Cf www.oldbaileyonline.org, trial reference t17680706-4 (1768) and t17700117-14 (1770).

6 All details are taken from the record of the trial at www.oldbailey online.org, trial reference t17700711-35.

7 *The Newgate Calendar* p.430.

8 All biographical details are taken from the Ordinary's Account, reference OA17520922.

9 Cf www.oldbaileyonline.org, trial reference t17501205-19 and t17501205-18 (1750) and t17520625-4 (1752).

10 *The London Mob* p.161.

11 All details are taken from the record of the trial at www.oldbailey online.org, trial reference t17520914-70.

12 Peter Linebaugh notes that Rag Fair was an area for fencing: 'Here 'pilferers' fenced their goods [...]' (*The London Hanged* p.265).

13 Cf www.oldbaileyonline.org, trial reference t17521026-50.

14 *Hanoverian London* p.97.

Chapter 4 – The Reverend Russen

1 All details are taken from the record of the trial at www.oldbailey online.org, reference t17771015-1.

2 *The Newgate Calendar* Knapp and Baldwin p.47.

3 *The Third Part of the Institutes of the Laws of England* p.60.

4 *A Treatise of the Pleas of the Crown: Volume One* p.439.

5 Ibid.

6 Ibid.

7 Details from *The Trials at Large of Joseph Merceron* W.B. Gurney.

8 *The Trials at Large of Joseph Merceron* vii.

9 Cf 'James Mayne [cce-id 70753], curate of Bethnal Green' Richard Palmer.

10 *The Trials at Large of Joseph Merceron* xiv.

11 Ibid p.2.

Chapter 5 – Bethnal House

1 *Bedlam* 125.

2 *The London Citizen Exceedingly Injured* Eighteenth Century Collections

Online Print Editions 2: all references are to this edition.

3 *Patterns of Madness* pp.93-4.

4 Ibid pp.8-9.

5 *Bedlam* p.121.

6 Ibid p.125.

7 *Annual Register*, 1772 (ed. Thomas English) 90-91: cf Arnold *Bedlam* p.126.

8 Details from Robinson and Chesshyre *The Green* pp.11-13.

9 *Report, from the Committee of the House of Commons on Madhouses in England 1815*: all references are to this edition.

10 *First Report: Minutes of Evidence, Taken before the Select Committee Appointed to Consider the Provision Being Made for the Better Regulation of Madhouses in England 1816*: all references are to this edition.

11 *Affidavits Sworn Before Lord Ellenborough* p.2.

12 *Report from Select Committee on Pauper Lunatics in the County of Middlesex, and on Lunatic Asylums 1827*: all references are to this edition.

13 *Further Report* pp.86-9.

14 *A Mad House Transformed* p.267.

15 *Report of the Metropolitan Commissioners in Lunacy, to the Lord Chancellor* p.27.

Chapter 6 – Undone by Poverty

1 All details are taken from the record of the trial at www.oldbaileyonline.org, trial reference t17110516-38.

2 All details are taken from the record of the trial at www.oldbaileyonline.org, trial reference t17521026-45.

3 Biographical details are taken from *The Newgate Calendar* 173-4 and the Ordinary's Account (see note below).

4 Cf *The Gentlemen's Magazine* 1748 (ed. Edward Cave), p.225.

5 Cf the Ordinary's Account, www.oldbaileyonline.org, reference OA17521113.

6 *Hanoverian London* 84.

7 Cf Fishman *East End 1888* p.202: 'Locally, the crime of infanticide was legendary; [...]'.

8 *Hanoverian London* p.88.

9 *The London Hanged* p.259.

10 All details are taken from the record of the trial at www.oldbaileyonline.org, trial reference t17340227-32.

11 For more details cf www.workhouses.org.uk/BethnalGreen.

12 Cf the Ordinary's Account, www.oldbaileyonline.org, reference OA17340308.

13 *London Labour and the London Poor: A Selection* li.
14 All details are taken from the record of the trial of Elias and Mary Ann Lipman at www.oldbaileyonline.org, trial reference t18700815-645.
15 Cf www.oldbaileyonline.org, trial reference t18610408-362.
16 Cf Fishman *East End 1888* 25: the Tower Hamlets were to become 'an over-congested ghetto of displaced labour with housing at a premium'.
17 All details are taken from the record of the trial at www.oldbaileyonline.org, trial reference t18471025-2345.
18 All details are taken from the record of the trial at www.oldbaileyonline.org, trial reference t18480703-1716.
19 Cf *Fishman East End* 1888 pp.201-02: 'Given the over-congested conditions exacerbated by scarcity in domestic housing [...] children in poor families were exposed to the dangers of incestuous or other sexual assaults by adults'.

Chapter 7 – Recommended to Mercy
1 Homicide Act, 1957 Part I, 2 (1).
2 Cf www.oldbaileyonline.org, trial reference t18860111-136.
3 A territorial unit: cf
http://london.wikia.com/wiki/Tower_Hamlets_Rifles.
4 Cf Fishman *East End 1888* 203: Old Gravel Lane Bridge is a 'popular' suicide spot. The old bridge was replaced when the waterway was narrowed by footpaths, though the old walls survive.
5 Cf www.oldbaileyonline.org, trial reference t18700711-585.
6 *The Times* of 31 May 1870 cites him as saying 'his stepmother had behaved very cruelly to him and his sister, and he had no further statement or explanation' (cf www.victorianlondon.org/crime/stepneymurder.htm).
7 *The Glasgow Daily Herald* (ed. William Jack) Friday 3 June p.5.
8 *The Teesdale Mercury* (ed. Reginald Atkinson) Wednesday 8 June p.7.
9 Cf www.oldbaileyonline.org, trial reference t19000911-549.
10 For some of the acts who performed at Foresters, see Baker, *British Music Hall* pp.33-4, 36-7, 93-4, 174-5.
11 *Hanging in the Balance* p.79.
12 Ibid p.78.
13 More information about Foresters can be found at this site:
http://www.arthurlloyd.co.uk/Foresters.htm

Chapter 8 – The City's Violent Shadow
1 *East End 1888* p.26.
2 Ibid p.28.
3 Cf www.oldbaileyonline.org, trial reference

NOTES

t18690111-218
4 Inquest details reproduced at
www.casebook.org/official_documents/inquests/inquest_smith.html.
5 Inquest details reproduced at www.casebook. org/official_
documents/inquests/inquest_tabram.html.
6 Cf www.oldbaileyonline.org, trial reference t18881119-64.
7 *East End 1888* p.209.
8 Cf www.oldbaileyonline.org, trial reference t18500819-1508.
9 Cf www.oldbaileyonline.org, trial reference t18500204-460.
10 Cf www.oldbaileyonline.org, trial reference t18550129-231.
11 Cf Paterson *Voices from Dickens' London* p.221, which quotes a description
from *The Cornhill Magazine* 1863 of the 'classic' method of garrotting, which
is similar to that carried out here.
12 Cf www.oldbaileyonline.org, trial reference t18850518-362.
13 Cf www.oldbaileyonline.org, trial reference t18690920-859.
14 Cf www.oldbaileyonline.org, trial reference t18701024-862.
15 Cf www.oldbaileyonline.org, trial reference t18560915-893.
16 Cf www.oldbaileyonline.org, trial reference t18700404-308.
17 *East End 1888* p.183.
18 Ibid 191-2.
19 Cf www.oldbaileyonline.org, trial reference t18741214-96.
20 Cf www.oldbaileyonline.org, trial reference t18520405-424.
21 Cf www.oldbaileyonline.org, trial reference t18620818-902.

Chapter 9 – Poison for the Asking
1 Cf Liza Picard, *Victorian London* p.186: 'The adulteration of food was
becoming a scandal [...]'.
2 Cf ibid 331: 'An astonishing number of poisons were ready to a murderer's
hand in the average home [...]'.
3 *The Inheritor's Powder* p.95.
4 Cf www.childrenshomes.org.uk/EastLondonSB for the school's history.
5 Cf www.oldbaileyonline.org, trial reference t18730203-182.
6 Hempel tells of the poisoning in 1842 of Daniel Cox, where to punish him
for cadging drinks his beer was adulterated at times with various substances
until he was given a lethal overdose of Epsom salts: 'the joke had gone too far'
(*The Inheritor's Powder* p.46).
7 Cf www.childrenshomes.org.uk/MiddlesexBoysIS.
8 Cf www.oldbaileyonline.org, trial reference t18910209-215.
9 Cf www.oldbaileyonline.org, trial reference t18500819-1503.
10 Helen Scales explains in 'Chemistry World' (October 2013) that cantharidin
'inflames the gastrointestinal tract and, depending on the dose, can completely

strip away the stomach lining' (sourced on-line – see bibliography).
11 Cf www.oldbaileyonline.org, trial reference t18510818-1691.
12 *Victorian London* pp.231-2.
13 Seemingly the original 16 Batty Street was demolished in 1888 for flats to be built; the present-day 16 Batty Street (of three storeys, rather than two) is not where Lipski lived (cf Martin Friedland *The Trials of Israel Lipski* p.17).
14 Cf www.oldbaileyonline.org, trial reference t18870725-817.
15 *The Trials of Israel Lipski* pp.157-8 and 98 respectively.
16 Ibid pp.173-4.
17 Ibid p.170.
18 Ibid pp.203-04.

Bibliography

Anon – *Observations on the Ruinous Tendency of the Spitalfields Act to the Silk Manufacture of London* (London: J. and A. Arch, 1822)

Arnold, Catharine – *Bedlam: London and its Mad* (London: Simon and Schuster, 2008; repr. Pocket Books, 2009)

Atkinson, Reginald (ed.) *The Teesdale Mercury* 1870.

Baker, Richard Anthony – *British Music Hall: An Illustrated History* (Barnsley: Pen and Sword, 2014)

Block, Brian P. and Hostettler, John – *Hanging in the Balance: A History of the Abolition of Capital Punishment in Britain* (Hook, Hants: Waterside Press, 1997)

Boswell, James (ed.) *The Scots Magazine: Volume XXXIII* (Edinburgh: A. Murray and J. Cochrane, 1771)

Cave, Edward (ed.) *The Gentlemen's Magazine, and Historical Chronicle* Volume XVIII (London: Edward Cave, 1748)

Coke, Edward – *The Third Part of the Institutes of the Laws of England: Concerning High Treason, and other Pleas of the Crown, and Criminall Causes* (London: W. Lee and D. Pakeman, 1644; repr. W. Clarke and Sons, London, 1809)

Commons, House of – *Report, from the Committee of the House of Commons, on Madhouses in England; together with Minutes of Evidence and an Appendix* (London: Baldwin Craddock and Joy, and R. Hunter, 1815)

Commons, House of – *First Report: Minutes of Evidence, Taken before the Select Committee Appointed to Consider the Provision Being Made for the Better Regulation of Madhouses in England* (London: House of Commons, 1816).

Commons, House of – *Report from Select Committee on Pauper Lunatics in the County of Middlesex, and on Lunatic Asylums* (London: House of Commons, 1827)

Cruden, Alexander – *The London-Citizen Exceedingly Injured: Or a British Inquisition Display'd* The Second Edition (London: T. Cooper and A. Dodd, 1739; reprinted Michigan: Gale Eighteenth Century Collections Online, 2010)

Cox, Jane – *Old East Enders: A History of the Tower Hamlets* (Stroud, Glos: The History Press, 2013)

East, Edward Hyde – *A Treatise of the Pleas of the Crown* Volume One (London: J. Butterworth, 1803)

English, Thomas (ed.) – *The Annual Register; Or a View of the History, Politics and Literature for the Year 1771* (London: J. Dodsley 1772)

English, Thomas (ed.) – *The Annual Register; Or a View of the History, Politics and Literature for the Year 1772: The Fifth Edition* (London: J. Dodsley, 1795)

Farham, James (ed.) – *An Abstract of an Act of Parliament [...] Impowering the Magistrates therein Mentioned to Settle and Regulate the Prices of Journeymen Silk Weavers, Working within their Respective Jurisdictions* (London: James Farham, 1789)

Fishman, William J. – *East End 1888: A Year in a London Borough among the Labouring Poor* (London: Duckworth 1988)

Friedland, Martin L. – The Trials of Israel Lipski: A True Story of a Victorian Murder in the East End of London (New York: Beaufort Books, 1984)

Gurney, W.B. – *The Trials at Large of Joseph Merceron, Esq for Fraud, as Treasurer of the Poor Rate Funds of St Matthew Bethnal Green* (London: W. Wright, 1819)

Hempel, Sandra – *The Inheritor's Powder: A Cautionary Tale of Poison, Betrayal and Greed* (London: Weidenfeld and Nicolson, 2013; repr. London: Phoenix, 2014)

Hindley, Charles – *Curiosities of London Street Literature: Comprising 'Cocks' and 'Catchpennies'* (London: Reeves and Turner, 1871)

Hughson, David – *London; Being an Accurate History and Description of the British Metropolis and its Neighbourhood to Thirty Miles Extent, from an Actual Perambulation* Volume One (London: J. Stratford, 1805)

Hunt, John (ed.) – *The Examiner* No. 928, Monday 21 November 1825, 735-50.

Ingram, Allan (ed.) – *Patterns of Madness in the Eighteenth Century: A Reader* (Liverpool: Liverpool University Press, 1998)

Jack, William (ed.) *The Glasgow Daily Herald* 1870.

Kimber, Isaac and Kimber, Edward (eds.) *The London Magazine: Or Gentleman's Monthly Intelligencer, Volume XXXIX: For the Year 1770* (London: R. Baldwin, 1771.

Knapp, A and Baldwin, W – *The Newgate Calendar; Comprising Interesting Memoirs of the Most Notorious Characters who have been Convicted of Outrages on the Laws of England since the Commencement of the Eighteenth Century* Volume 2 (London: J. Robins and Co., 1825)

Linebaugh, Peter – *The London Hanged* (London: Verso, 2003)

Mayhew, Henry – *London Labour and the London Poor: A Selection by Rosemary O'Day and David Englander* (Ware, Herts: Wordsworth Editions, 2008)

Metropolitan Commissioners in Lunacy – *Report of the Metropolitan Commissioners in Lunacy, to the Lord Chancellor* (London: Bradbury and Evans, 1844)

Metropolitan Commissioners in Lunacy – *Further Report of the Commissioners in Lunacy, to the Lord Chancellor* (London: Shaw and Sons, 1847)

Mitford, John – *A Description of the Crimes and Horrors in the Interior of Warburton's Private Mad-House at Hoxton, Commonly Called Whitmore House* (London: Benbow, 1825)

BIBLIOGRAPHY

Murphy, Elaine – 'A Mad House Transformed' *Notes and Records of the Royal Society* 58 (3) 2004, 267-281.

Palmer, Richard – 'James Mayne [cce-id 70753], curate of Bethnal Green', *Clergy of the Church of England Database* Online Journal N&Q 2, 2008 (www.theclergydatabase.org.uk/cce_n2.html)

Paterson, Michael – *Voices from Dickens' London* (Newton Abbot: David and Charles, 2006)

Picard, Liza – *Victorian London: The Life of a City 1840-1870* (London: Weidenfeld and Nicolson, 2005; repr. London: Phoenix, 2006)

Robinson, A.J. and Chesshyre, D.H.B. – *The Green: A History of the Heart of Bethnal Green and the Legend of the Blind Beggar* (London: London Borough of Tower Hamlets Central Library, 1978, repr. 1986)

Rogers, J.W. – *A Statement of the Cruelties, Abuses and Frauds, which are Practised in Mad-Houses* (London: Wilson, 1816)

Rudé, George – *Hanoverian London 1714-1808* (London: Martin Secker and Warburg, 1971; repr. Stroud, Glos: Sutton Publishing Ltd, 2003)

Scales, Helen – 'Spanish Fly' *Chemistry World* Podcast (www. rsc.org/ chemistryworld/2013/10/spanish-fly-cantharidin-podcast)

Shoemaker, Robert – *The London Mob: Violence and Disorder in Eighteenth-Century England* (London: Hambledon Continuum, 2004, repr. 2007)

Talbot, Matthew and Humieres, Mary – *Affidavits Sworn Before Lord Ellenborough in Refutation of the Testimony of John Wilson Rogers and Mary Humieres* (London: 1816)

On-Line Resources
Arthur Lloyd: The Music Hall and Theatre History Site: http://www.arthur lloyd.co.uk

Casebook: Jack the Ripper: http://www.casebook.org

Children's Homes: http://www.childrenshomes.org.uk

The London Wikia: http://london.wikia.com/wiki/London_Wiki

Old London Maps: http://mapco.net/london.htm

The Proceedings of the Old Bailey, 1674-1913: http://www.oldbaileyonline.org

Pubs History: http://pubshistory.com

Tower Hamlets History On-Line: http://www.mernick.org.uk/thhol

UK Public General Acts: http://www.legislation.gov.uk/ukpga

The Victorian Dictionary: http://www.victorianlondon.org

The Workhouse: The Story of an Institution: http://www.workhouses.org.uk

Index

186

INDEX

187